VLADIMIR LENIN AND THE RUSSIAN REVOLUTION

**Elizabeth Schmermund
and Judith Edwards**

Enslow Publishing
101 W. 23rd Street
Suite 240
New York, NY 10011
USA

enslow.com

Published in 2016 by Enslow Publishing, LLC
101 W. 23rd Street, Suite 240, New York, NY 10011

Library of Congress Cataloging-in-Publication Data

Schmermund, Elizabeth, author.
Vladimir Lenin and the Russian Revolution / Elizabeth Schmermund and Judith Edwards.
   pages cm. — (People and events that changed the world)
Includes bibliographical references and index.
Summary: "Describes the life of Vladimir Lenin and his philosophies which led to the Russian revolution in the 20th century"— Provided by publisher.
Audience: Grade 7 to 8.
ISBN 978-0-7660-7414-9
1. Soviet Union—History—Revolution, 1917-1921—Juvenile literature. 2. Lenin, Vladimir Il'ich, 1870-1924—Juvenile literature. I. Edwards, Judith, 1940- author. II. Title.
DK265.S3545 2016
947.084'1092—dc23
                              2015025537

Printed in the United States of America

To Our Readers: We have done our best to make sure all website addresses in this book were active and appropriate when we went to press. However, the author and the publisher have no control over and assume no liability for the material available on those websites or on any websites they may link to. Any comments or suggestions can be sent by e-mail to customerservice@enslow.com.

Portions of this book originally appeared in the book *Lenin and the Russian Revolution in World History*.

Photo Credits: Cover, p. 1 Fine Art Images/Heritage Images/Hulton Archive/Getty Images (Vladimir Lenin), EdwardSV/Shutterstock.com (series logo background and headers throughout book); p. 4 Hulton Archive/Getty Images; p. 9 Wikipedia/Lenin Age 4.jpg/public domain; pp. 11, 34, 44, 51, 92 Sovfoto/Universal Images Group/Getty Images; p. 15 Photo12/ Universal Images Group/Getty Images; p. 18 DEA / A. DAGLI ORTI/DeAgostini/Getty Images; p. 21 DEA / J. E. BULLOZ/DeAgostini/Getty Images; p. 26 Roger Viollet/Getty Images; p. 31 Popperfoto/Getty Images; p. 40 Hans Wild/The LIFE Picture Collection/Getty Images; p. 48 The Print Collector/ Hulton Archive/Getty Images; pp. 53, 58, 62, 82, 85 ullstein bild/ullstein bild via Getty Images; p. 67 Apic/ Hulton Archive/Getty Images; p. 69 FPG/Hulton Archive/ Archive Photos Getty Images; pp. 72, 88, 108 Fine Art Images/Heritage Images/Hulton Archive/Getty Images; pp. 75, 106, 110 Universal History Archive/ Universal Images Group/ Getty Images; p. 77 Archiv Gerstenberg/ullstein bild via Getty Images; p. 97 Ann Ronan Pictures/Print Collector/Hulton Archives/Getty Images; p. 99 Keystone/ Hulton Archive/Getty Images; p. 113 © AP Images.

CONTENTS

Vladimir Lenin

CHAPTER 1

A Revolutionary Beginning

"Don't you know anything?" Moisei Bronksy shouted at his friend, Vladimir Ilych Lenin. It was March 15, 1917, and Lenin and his wife, Nadezdha Krupskaya, were at home in Zurich, Switzerland when Bronsky stormed in.[1] Lenin hadn't yet heard what Bronsky already knew: Revolution had finally broken out in Russia. Upon hearing the good news, Lenin and his wife rushed outside to find a newspaper.

These exiles from the Russian government were not just concerned for their homeland. Lenin had spent sixteen years of his adult life either in exile, imprisoned, or away from Russia. He had spent those years writing, giving speeches, organizing political parties, and waiting eagerly for the day when there would be a revolt against the oppressive government of the Russian tsar (ruler).

Lenin had worked not just for revolution, but for the complete overthrow of the Russian government, which did not allow ordinary people any say in making the laws of the country. Lenin wanted to replace the tsar not with a democracy, but with a socialist system, soon to be called Communism. He believed that a Communist government

5

would put workers in control of their own destiny. Lenin insisted that these workers would be led by a small number of dedicated, professional revolutionaries. His own party, called the Bolsheviks, from the Russian word for "majority," would lead the way to this coming "dictatorship of the proletariat"—dictatorship of the workers.

Now the time had come, and Lenin was far from Russia. World War I was raging, and he would have to cross enemy territory—through Austria-Hungary or Germany—to get to the Russian capital. He had to reach St. Petersburg, which had been newly renamed Petrograd.

Lenin explored several options. Perhaps he could start his journey through France or Great Britain, rather than enemy countries. However, these countries, which were relying on Russia as an ally in the war, were not likely to help Lenin—an outspoken opponent of Russian participation in the war—return home.[2] Lenin considered all possible routes home, both practical and fantastical. The situation was critical. He had to return to Russia if he wanted the Bolsheviks to have the deciding influence in shaping the outcome of the revolution.

Germany—Russia's enemy in the ongoing war—was quite willing to help Lenin. The Germans knew all about Lenin's hatred of the tsarist government and his wish for Russia to lose the war so the government would fail. The Germans thought that transporting Russian revolutionaries like Lenin back to Russia just might help Germany win the war. Secrecy was important. The Germans did not want their enemies to know what they were doing and try to stop them. Likewise, Lenin and his fellow Russian exiles did not want the Russian people to know that they were being helped by their German enemies.

Primary Source—
Letter from V.I. Lenin to
Inessa Armand, 1917

We in Zurich are in a state of agitation today: there is a telegram in *Zürcher Post* and in *Neue Zürcher Zeitung* of March 15 that in Russia the revolution was victorious in Petrograd on March 14 after three days of struggle, that 12 members of the Duma are in power and the ministers have all been arrested. If the Germans are not lying, then it's true. That Russia has for the last few days been on the eve of revolution is beyond doubt . . . .[3]

Lenin, the Bolshevik leader the Germans wanted most to send back to Russia, would be permitted, through complex and devious negotiations, to choose those who would return to Russia with him. A sealed train would transport the revolutionaries. They would travel from Switzerland, across Germany, into Sweden, and then south through Finland to reach the Russian frontier.

When the thirty-two Russian exiles started out on this highly secret journey, they had no idea if they would make it all the way back to Russia. Even if they did arrive, they could not be sure what kind of reception they would receive. Most of all, they were concerned about how the Provisional Government—which had recently been put in place temporarily to replace the tsar—and other revolutionary groups would feel about the return of the famous Vladimir Ilych Lenin.[4]

The Ulyanov Family

In 1870 Simbirsk was a bustling port town along the Volga River, east of Moscow. The population of Simbirsk was about forty-three thousand and most of its residents depended upon peasant agriculture. The Ulyanov family moved there several months before their son, Vladimir Ilych, later known as Vladimir Lenin, was born. It was in this city that the Ulyanov family rose to prominence, from peasants to more prominent figures of Simbirsk.[1]

The Family Tree

The Ulyanov family was living comfortably in Simbirsk when Vladimir Ilych Ulyanov, the third of six children, was born on April 10, 1870. (His birthdate was April 10 on the old-style Julian calendar that Russia used at the time. On the more modern Gregorian calendar used by most other countries, his birthdate was April 22. Unless otherwise stated, all dates mentioned will follow the new-style calendar.)

Ilya Nikolayevich, the new baby's father, was a mathematics teacher and an inspector of schools for the ministry (department) of education. Ilya's father had been a tailor, the son of a serf. (Russian peasants, who were required to give part of their farm crop or any other earnings to the large landowners on whose land they lived, were called serfs.) Ilya's mother was Swedish.

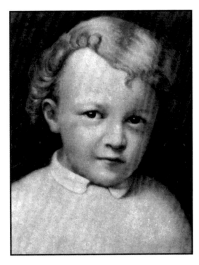

Vladimir Ulyanov, age four.

As a child, Vladimir had very dark, slanting eyes; high cheekbones; and a broad, flat nose, all of which gave him an Asiatic appearance. In fact, his great-grandmother was Kalmyk, one of the Mongolian peoples who were accepted into greater Russia when they were baptized as Orthodox Christians. Vladimir's mother, Maria Alexandrovna, was the daughter of Alexander Blank, a German Jewish doctor who also became a baptized Christian. Becoming a Christian, no matter what one's original religion, was the only road to social and professional acceptance in Russia at the time. Dr. Blank married a German woman who was very well-educated. He eventually bought a thousand-acre estate in the village of Kokushkino.

The child Vladimir, who would later become the father of the Russian Revolution, was German, Swedish, and Kalmyk. According to historian Dmitri Volkogonov, "There was not a drop of Russian blood in him."[2] Vladimir Ilych Ulyanov, who later called himself Lenin, had a family tree as diverse as any American's. After the revolution, Lenin's family background would be covered up by Communist party leaders "because it was felt that the leader of the Russian revolution must be a Russian."[3]

Early Education

As a small child, Vladimir had difficulty learning to walk, and sometimes threw tantrums. He had a bad habit of breaking things on purpose.[4] Even so, his quickness of mind and frequent sweetness made him a favorite at home.[5] He became an excellent student, particularly interested in languages.

When Vladimir's father was promoted to director of schools for the whole province of Simbirsk, the family moved to a larger home. It was a sunny house with many rooms that were filled with books and plants. Vladimir covered the walls of his room with maps.[6] Outside, there were orchards that held apple and cherry trees.

The Ulyanovs spent summers at their estate in Kokushkino in the province of Kazan. One-fifth of the property was owned by Vladimir's mother, Maria Alexandrovna, and the rest by her siblings. Here, as well as in Simbirsk, Maria Alexandrovna enjoyed growing flowers with her children's help.[7]

The family had servants, including a private tutor who remained with the Ulyanovs until the children entered school around the age of nine. It was not unusual for children of well-off Russian people to enter school late. Private tutors and parents usually gave children their early education. The secondary school, which prepared students for examinations, was called a gymnasium. Upon entering the gymnasium, there was a wide selection of subjects to choose from and to learn in detail. Even before going to school, Vladimir had won a reputation as a hard worker.[8]

The Ulyanov Family

The Ulyanov family in Simbirsk in 1879. Parents, Maria Alexandrovna and Ilya Nikolayevich, are seated. Children are, standing from left to right: Olga, Alexander, and Anna. Other children, seated from left to right, are Maria (on mother's lap), Dmitri, and Vladimir.

A boy who shared a desk with Vladimir said, "At school Ulyanov differed considerably from all of us, his comrades. Neither in the lower forms nor later did he take part in the childish and youthful games and pranks, always keeping to himself, busy either with his studies or some written work."[9]

The biggest influence on Vladimir was his older brother, Alexander. There were four years separating them. Alexander was very much the leader at home. He edited a family weekly newspaper to which he expected his four brothers and sisters to contribute.[10] Alexander was a brilliant student in school, especially interested in natural science. He was a generous and polite young man, who preferred to keep his private thoughts private. The young Vladimir adored him and tried to copy Alexander's even-tempered discipline.[11] The brothers were close during Lenin's early childhood, but their very different personalities had drawn them apart by the time Alexander left for college.

Double Tragedy

The happy provincial life of the Ulyanov family ended abruptly with two incidents. First, Lenin's father, Ilya Ulyanov, died unexpectedly in January 1886, when Lenin was just fifteen years old. Because he had been removed from his post as director of schools with no explanation the previous year, the father had not left much money behind. Maria Alexandrovna Ulyanova had to apply to the state for a pension, which was granted on request to people who worked for the state service, to support her family.

A year later, Alexander, who was then a college student, was arrested and put on trial for plotting to assassinate the tsar. Despite the pleas of his mother, Alexander was executed. Vladimir and Alexander's sister Anna had been visiting Alexander when he was arrested. She was arrested, too, but was released after Alexander's execution. She was told, however, that she would be watched by the police and would have to move to the family estate at Kokushkino. The Ulyanov family, in Simbirsk, was shunned by neighbors.

This was a shocking and terrible blow to the family. None of the Ulyanovs had known that Alexander, the gentle and gifted student who had received a gold medal for outstanding work when he graduated high school, was involved in revolutionary activity.[12] For Vladimir, life would never be the same.

Primary Source— Alexander Ulyanov's Speech at His Trial, 1887

Terror . . . is the only form of defense by which a minority strong only in its spiritual strength and the consciousness of its righteousness [can combat] the physical power of the majority . . . Among the Russian people there will always be found many people who are so devoted to their ideas and who feel so bitterly the unhappiness of their country that it will not be a sacrifice for them to offer their lives . . . [13]

The Seeds of Revolution

For much of the nineteenth century, Russia was pulled between traditional values and modern reforms. By 1815 Russia was a world power, but it lagged behind other nations because it relied on serfdom. Serfdom is when serfs, or peasant farmers, are bound to the land of a wealthy family for whom they work. In Russia at this time, democratic freedoms did not exist. The tsar was the absolute ruler of the nation. Yet by the middle of the century, although the tsar still had popular support, many Russians were calling for reforms.

History of Russia

Russia developed at a different rate and along different lines compared to Western Europe. The Russian Empire ranged across two continents—from the Gulf of Finland in the west and east to the Pacific Ocean; from the frozen Arctic in the north and south to the borders of what were then Turkey, Persia, and Afghanistan. This empire was larger than the ancient Roman Empire at its peak. It comprised 8.5 million

A Russian peasant couple in the nineteenth century. For centuries, the Russians used serfs, or peasants, to work land that was owned by the nobility.

square miles, or one sixth of the total land surface of the earth.

Feudalism—the system based on the relationship between landowners and the peasants who lived on their land—was slow to emerge in Russia. This was because of the vast expanse of free land and the many different ethnic groups. The development toward modern culture also passed Russia by, mainly because Russia was not being used by other countries as a significant trade route by the thirteenth century. As a result, while the great art and new ideas of the Renaissance were flourishing in Western Europe, Russia remained isolated.

When the Mongols and Tatars (Asian peoples) invaded Russia during the thirteenth and fourteenth centuries, the remaining trade centers were destroyed, but the invaders were able to govern large areas of land. They were willing to tolerate local customs, religions, and governments—as long as the local rulers and military establishment were submissive to Mongol dominance and paid tribute.[1]

As the Mongols gradually faded from power, the Russian nobility acted on what it had learned from its conquerors about government administration. In 1640, after instituting the Ulozhenie law code, which made serfdom a legal category binding a class of people to the land on which they lived, Moscow was made a holy city. This move, which made Moscow the home of the head of state and military organizations, was done with the cooperation of the Russian Orthodox Church. From the capital at Moscow, the tsar now ruled absolutely across the vast empire.

Serfdom

The masses in Russia came to think of the tsar as their "father" and the system as their caretaker. Threats to the empire from countries in Western Europe continually strengthened loyalty to the state and the tsar. Serfdom, which kept peasants from moving from province to province within Russia, also helped stabilize the empire. The tax collector and the army recruiter were better able to keep track of where to find each person. Each village was responsible collectively for its share of tax money and its quota of soldiers to be drafted for war. Serfdom was solidified in Russia at the very same time it was declining in England and France.

The great problem for Russia was that its rulers lacked the technique and the manpower to rule their huge empire. Unlike the civil service systems of other countries, the Russian bureaucracy generally operated as "the personal staff of the monarch rather than as the civil service of the nation," according to historian Richard Pipes.[2]

Modernization

In the seventeenth century, Tsar Peter the Great decided Russia needed to catch up with the rest of Europe, culturally and militarily. To do this, he brought in industry and introduced European culture to his reluctant nobility, who rebelled at the changes as much as they dared. Peter's changes were made not to help the peasants, who were left no better off than before, but because of the needs of the state.[3]

Western ideas infiltrated and changed the Russian feudal empire over the next century. A few dozen officers, most of them major landowners, rebelled briefly in December 1825.

The Russian Empire grew considerably under the rule of Tsar Peter the Great. The leader also pushed for the modernization of many of the country's social and political systems.

They hoped to form a constitutional monarchy. Though this Decembrist Revolt was quickly suppressed by the military, it led the government to rely more heavily on a professional bureaucracy, lessening the influence of the nobility.

By the time Tsar Alexander II freed the serfs in 1861, Russia was no longer totally isolated from modern ideas. In response to these changes, the weakened landowners either became reactionary (meaning they did not want reform) or joined the new intelligentsia—writers, professors, and students who wished to liberalize Russian laws.

Alexander II wanted not only to free the serfs but also to engage the intellectuals in helping to expand the state's European institutions. In 1864 Alexander created the *zemstva*, the Russian word for local government institutions. These were set up to help Russia end its feudal system. The zemstva increased political awareness among the landowners and hinted at the beginnings of a middle class. New jobs were created as Alexander sought to bring about greater responsibility among the people in charge of new government bodies. The tsar made changes in the system of law, in the universities, and in censorship. His aim was to create a representative government, under the tsar's leadership. Not all Russians were happy about this—particularly nobles who stood to lose their hereditary titles.

Assassination and Revolutionary Ideas

Revolutionaries—including former nobles, students, and discouraged members of the civil service—turned to terrorism to hasten changes that would help the former serfs. Tsar Alexander II approved a constitution on March 13, 1881. That same day, before it could take effect, he was assassinated.

Alexander II's son, Tsar Alexander III, returned to the strict line against political expression and independent social activity that had been the rule under his father's reign. At the same time, he wanted to continue Russia's modernization and industrialization. As usual when reforms came to tsarist Russia, peasants were the last to benefit from them. The authority of landowners was replaced by communes. Peasants were given plots of land that were partially owned by the state on which to grow crops. The communes were extremely inefficient. In order to be fair in distributing the limited land within each commune, historian W. Bruce Lincoln explains,

> Peasant communes divided their holdings into many small strips according to the land's fertility, water supply, and distance from the village, and then assigned to every household the use of a certain number of strips depending upon how many holdings of each family thus lay scattered over the commune's entire domain.[4]

This system meant that farm tools had to be moved from strip to strip, wasting valuable time. Another problem was that the amount of land allotted to each family changed as the number of family members grew or diminished. Since many families had members die or leave to obtain industrial work in the cities, there was often not enough land for the peasants to produce their own food. And because they did not really own the land, there was no incentive to improve it. The soil was often ruined when it was used too many times for the same crop.

Vladimir's brother Alexander became involved in an unsuccessful plot to assassinate Tsar Alexander III, seen here.

Primary Source— Alexander II's Emancipation Manifesto, 1861

. . . Examining the condition of classes and professions comprising the state, We became convinced that the present state legislation favours the upper and middle classes, defines their obligations, rights, and privileges, but does not equally favour the serfs, so designated because in part from old laws and in part from custom they have been hereditarily subjected to the authority of landowners, who in turn were obligated to provide for their well-being. . . . The way was opened for an arbitrariness burdensome for the peasants and detrimental to their welfare, causing them to be indifferent to the improvement of their own existence. . . . [T]he serfs will receive in time the full rights of free rural inhabitants. . . . At the same time, they are granted the right to purchase their domicile, and, with the consent of the nobles, they may acquire in full ownership the arable lands and other properties which are allotted them for permanent use. Following such acquisition of full ownership of land, the peasants will be freed from their obligations to the nobles for the land thus purchased and will become free peasant landowners.[5]

As the peasant's lot worsened, so did the repression of intellectual thought. Instead of continuing the permissive climate Alexander II had created for intellectuals, there was new censorship, particularly of students. Demonstrations were not allowed, and the police, who had allowed assembly during the reign of Alexander II, were active again in ending public political gatherings.

But the gates had already been thrown open. Democratic ideas were filtering through, even to partially educated Russians. The idea of revolution had been planted.

Terrorism

Into this climate came the idealistic student Alexander Ulyanov. The older brother of Vladimir Ulyanov had, at first, ignored the attempts of other students to get him involved in revolutionary activity. In fact, the revolutionary movement that brought about the assassination of Alexander II had been virtually wiped out by the time Alexander Ulyanov was a college student. Eventually, however, he became involved in a small—and very ineffectual—plot to assassinate Tsar Alexander III. Alexander Ulyanov became the revolutionary group's chief maker of explosives. When they were arrested, several of the conspirators lied about their involvement or renounced their cause to receive lighter sentences. Alexander, true to his honest nature, told his judges: "There is no finer death than death for one's country's sake; such a death holds no terror for sincere and honest men. I had but one aim: to help the unfortunate Russian people."[6] Alexander Ulyanov was put to death for his crime.

A Revolutionary Is Born

After Alexander's execution, the local and state governments made sure that everyone knew about Alexander's crime. In the town of Simbirsk, posters were hung up featuring Alexander and articles were written about him in the local newspaper. Townspeople distanced themselves from the Ulyanov family. Yet, shortly after Alexander's execution, Vladimir Ulyanov graduated from high school at the head of his class. He received the highest grades possible in all of his subjects, and received a gold medal for his studies, just as his older brother had received before him. For some time after graduation, Vladimir could not decide where to go to school. Finally, he decided on his father's alma mater, Kazan University, where he would study law. This choice surprised and worried those closest to him, who couldn't understand why Vladimir, who had always been interested in literature and languages, would want to study law and politics after his brother's execution.

Brief College Days

Alexander's death affected Vladimir deeply. There is no proof, however, as some writers have suggested, that he became "Lenin the revolutionary" then and there. He did choose law and political economy as his major subjects, which familiarized him with any revolutionary activity that might exist at Kazan. But even when he met informally with other law students, he was watched by the authorities.[1] Vladimir Ulyanov was present during a minor demonstration by students, though he was not actually seen to participate. Nevertheless, the fact that he was Alexander's brother led to his expulsion from Kazan. Not only was he expelled, but he was, like his sister Anna, confined to the family estate at Kokushkino.

If the authorities had thought about it, they might have realized that expelling this bright student just because his brother had been executed for revolutionary activity might have made it even more likely that Vladimir would become a revolutionary. "By thus ostracizing him, the tsarist authorities were steadily narrowing Lenin's range of choices. His solidarity with his dead brother became more firmly fixed," historian Dmitri Volkogonov states.[2]

Both Lenin—a name he would adopt permanently in 1901—and his mother wrote respectful letters to the school authorities, trying to get him reinstated at Kazan. They were unsuccessful. Lenin also wrote letters requesting permission to attend a foreign university. These requests, too, were denied.

The Influence of Marxism

The family bought a small farm thirty miles from Kokushkino in 1889, in the province of Samara. Lenin completed his "exile" in this remote part of Russia, devoting himself to reading anything social and political. It was during this time that he first read Karl Marx's *Das Kapital.*

During the time that Lenin was expelled from university, he began reading the works of German revolutionary Karl Marx.

Primary Source— From Karl Marx's *Capital*: Critique of Political Economy, 1867

Let us now picture to ourselves, by way of change, a community of free individuals, carrying on their work with the means of production in common, in which the labour-power of all the different individuals is consciously applied as the combined labour-power of the community. . . . The total product of our community is a social product. One portion serves as fresh means of production and remains social. But another portion is consumed by the members as means of subsistence. A distribution of this portion amongst them is consequently necessary. The mode of this distribution will vary with the productive organisation of the community.[3]

Karl Marx was a German Jew who believed in a classless society. He and his colleague, Friedrich Engels, believed that capitalism—the economic system in which businesses are owned and run by private individuals, leading to competition in a free market—allows business owners to exploit workers. Therefore, one class (the bourgeoisie, or middle-class business owners) oppresses another class (the proletariat, or workers). Because European countries (except for Russia) lived under this long accepted capitalist system, the only way to overthrow it and to win equality for all people, Marx argued, was by revolution—not by dialogue and laws, but by the forceful (if necessary) overthrow of capitalism.[4]

Marx taught that history showed that feudalism ended when power was taken from the ruling class of landowners and nobles by the capitalist middle class. The next stage of social change would come when the workers took power from the middle class. As Lenin read Marx's ideas, he realized that there was no real middle class in Russia. The tsar and those connected to him were still in power. Against whom, therefore, would the revolution be directed if it took place in Russia?[5]

A novelist named Nikolai Chernyshevski was very influential in shaping Lenin's interpretation of Marx. Of Chernyshevski's novel *What Is to Be Done?*, Lenin wrote, "It is a work that gives one a charge for a whole life." Two beliefs from this popular late-nineteenth-century book captured the mind of the extraordinarily disciplined young man whom the government had treated badly. According to historian Elyse Topalian, one was that "the individual is the potential holder of great power . . . that can influence events or even alter the course of history; and second, that total dedication to one's ideals means that any path toward achieving one's ends is valid and justifiable."[6]

Law Studies

While reading almost nonstop and absorbing new ideas that would, indeed, change the course of history, the young Lenin, not yet twenty-one, persisted in his attempt to continue his university studies. Finally, thanks to his mother's efforts, Lenin was given permission to take the law examinations given by St. Petersburg University. He was allowed to study by himself and take the examinations when he felt ready.

Working intensively for a year at home—at a four-year college course in law—Lenin passed his exams with perfect grades. In November 1891, when Lenin was twenty-one, he received his diploma from St. Petersburg University. With a little more political wrangling from his mother, he was awarded the "Certificate of Loyalty and Good Character." Without this endorsement, he could not have practiced law, despite his first-class diploma.[7]

This amazing accomplishment, evidence of Lenin's intelligence and self-discipline, led to a disappointingly short and undistinguished legal career. In the years after getting his law degree, Lenin was really turning his attention to learning more about Marxism. He was gradually trying to be accepted as an important agitator in revolutionary circles.

The Plight of the Peasants

At the same time Lenin earned his degree, the famine of 1891 started because of the policies of Tsar Alexander's finance minister, Ivan Vyshnegradskii. To increase Russia's gold reserves, the country had to create a better balance of trade with other countries. Since industrial growth had not managed to produce large amounts of marketable goods, Russia needed to export more food to achieve that trade balance. This food would come from the peasants who grew it. Vyshnegradskii proclaimed, "We may not eat enough, but we will export."[8] Because of his policies, whole villages starved. Then, an unusually severe winter in 1890–1891, followed by an unusually hot, dry summer, continued the disaster. Weakened by hunger, more of the rural peasant population was wiped out by disease.

This famine brought about a severe split in the viewpoints of those who were working for social reform. Georgi Plekhanov, a revolutionary leader who had been in exile from Russia since 1881, believed that bringing relief to famine victims only helped the government continue its poor management. He urged revolutionaries to use their energy instead to expose the weaknesses of the government, which would lead to its eventual overthrow. Moderates, on the other hand, argued that helping the government end the famine would lead to eventual reform, because it would increase the peasants' influence.

The early writings of Nikolai Chernyshevski and Plekhanov shaped the beliefs of the majority of young Marxists. Lenin's brother had been executed by the tsarist government, his family was shunned by the liberal intelligentsia, and Lenin had been denied the company of professors and fellow students during his college years. Though he read widely and formed his ideas not only from Marxist philosophers, Lenin was "never able to assimilate [take as his own] the ideas of the liberals, who proclaimed the rule of law, or the 'Economists,' who wanted the workers to flourish, or the Western democrats, who put parliamentary government above all else."[9] According to historian Dmitri Volkogonov, "For Lenin, Marxism meant above all one thing, and that was revolution. It was the revolutionary message of the doctrine that attracted him in the first place. . . . Lenin's 'discovery' of Marxism was thus extremely selective; he saw in it only what he wanted to see."[10]

Georgi Plekhanov, an early hero of Lenin's, was one of the first Russians to call himself a Marxist.

Lenin in Exile

Lenin understood that, while the peasant masses were suffering under serfdom, it would be hard to organize them in the fight for revolution. This was not only because so many peasant farmers worked hard to avoid starvation during the famine and did not have the time for a Marxist revolution. It was also because, Lenin believed, the peasants were isolated from the real cause of their oppression—capitalism.[1] Instead, Lenin wanted to focus on organizing urban workers, called the proletariat, who better understood why revolution was necessary.

Lenin moved from Samara to St. Petersburg in the summer of 1893. Though he worked in a law office, his main activity in St. Petersburg was organizing in Marxist circles. Even at legal meetings, he talked about Marxism. Because of his activity, he was watched by the police. Lenin continued to write and talk about his main themes from Marxism: "classes and class struggle, and the dictatorship of the proletariat."[2]

Marxist Group and Arrest

Another revolutionary, Julius Tsderbaum, also called Yuli Martov, had arrived in St. Petersburg in 1893 after a short stint in prison for agitating. Lenin's association with Martov led to the formation of a dedicated Marxist group. In 1895, Lenin was granted a visa to go abroad. He made a brief visit to the Marxist leader in exile, Plekhanov. The famous revolutionary was impressed with Lenin's dedication.

Back in St. Petersburg, in addition to attending many secret Marxist meetings, Lenin and some of his colleagues began handing out Marxist propaganda in factories. He hoped that "this would bring them [the workers] in conflict with the state authorities and in this manner politicize them."[3] Lenin was disappointed in the workers' response. There was no freedom of speech in Russia, and the workers were reluctant to risk their jobs and their lives by going along with these revolutionary ideas.

Lenin himself was arrested in 1895 for his propaganda activity. He spent a year in prison in St. Petersburg. There, he spent most of his time doing research for a book he would later write. One of the people who supplied him with research materials was Nadezhda Krupskaya, a young Marxist teacher he had met while attending political meetings.

Marriage in Siberia

Lenin was exiled to Siberia in 1897, after first visiting his sick mother for a week. Once again, his mother helped him by petitioning the government for all kinds of leniency. Lenin was allowed to travel to Siberia alone, and he was permitted to stay in a more southern Siberian province because of his supposed ill health.[4]

Nadezhda Krupskaya, herself arrested and exiled to Siberia, was granted permission to be transferred to Shushenskoe, where Lenin was, to serve her term. She and

Lenin's mug shot, taken after his arrest in 1895.

Primary Source—
Letter From V.I. Lenin to
His Mother, 1898

Our wedding has been somewhat delayed. I handed in an application for the necessary papers to be sent to us a month ago, and myself went to the police chief in Minusinsk to enquire the reason for the delay. It turned out that the "status sheet" has not yet (Siberian ways!) been received in Minusinsk although I have been here in exile over a year (the "status sheet" is a paper identifying the exiled person and without it the police chief knows nothing about me and cannot give me any certificate). It has to be obtained from the Krasnoyarsk prison authorities—I am afraid the police chief will not hurry with this. In any case there cannot be a wedding earlier than July. I asked him to allow the people to come from Tes to my wedding and he refused outright on the grounds that one political exile in Minusinsk (Raichin) got leave of absence to go to a village last March and disappeared. . . .[5]

Lenin were married in July 1898. Although there appeared to be some genuine affection between the couple, it was Krupskaya's willingness to be a dedicated revolutionary and a devoted follower of Lenin that cemented their relationship right from the beginning.[6] Being an exile in Siberia at that time meant freedom to pursue revolutionary study and writing. Books and articles arrived by mail, and Lenin grew healthy on a routine of reading, writing, and walking in the clear air. His wife became his valued assistant. She helped him with editing and listened as he completed the chapters of his first major book, *The Development of Capitalism in Russia.*[7]

The Role of Workers

Meanwhile, the revolutionaries who had not been arrested were experiencing problems. Although they had formed a group called the Russian Social Democratic Labor Party (RSDLP), they were continually watched by the police. Once again, because of fear of the police—and even of change itself—the workers did not welcome their ideas. However, the idea of trade unions—instead of revolution—as a means of lessening the workers' plight was gaining ground with the help of liberals.

Lenin felt that if the workers were not organized by revolutionaries, they would simply give in to capitalism and continue to be oppressed. While he was in Siberia, Lenin wrote another book and borrowed Nikolai Chernyshevski's title *What Is to Be Done?* Lenin's book, which would be published in Germany in 1902, solidified his revolutionary theory that, "unless the workers were led by a socialist party composed of professional revolutionaries, they would betray their class interests (as understood by socialists) and

Primary Source—From Lenin's *What Is to Be Done?*

[T]o concentrate all secret functions in the hands of as small a number of professional revolutionaries as possible does not mean that the latter will do the thinking for all and that the crowd will not take an active part in the movement. On the contrary, the crowd will advance from its ranks increasing numbers of professional revolutionaries, for it will know that it is not enough for a few students and workingmen, waging economic war, to gather together and form a committee, but that it takes years to train professional revolutionaries; the crowd will think not of primitive ways but of training professional revolutionaries.[8]

sell out."[9] For Lenin, this meant that the workers simply would never even understand their own interests as a class. They needed to be taught by professionals, like himself and his party. These beliefs would eventually lead to the worst excesses of the Russian Revolution.

Growing Pains in the Party

After finishing his term of exile on February 10, 1900, Lenin was allowed to leave Siberia but was forbidden from living in any major cities or university towns. This did not dissuade him from his work, however. Choosing to settle in a small town that was close to St. Petersburg, Lenin began to secretly enter large cities and meet with revolutionary groups.[1] He announced to them his plan to start an underground newspaper, called *Iskra* or "The Spark," and asked for their support.[2] These dedicated revolutionaries would help carry the paper around Russia and gather more people interested in their cause.

Iskra would have to be written and printed outside of Russia. While Lenin was in Siberia, there had been wide-scale arrests of the remaining Marxist intellectuals in St. Petersburg. In addition, a document called "Credo of the Young," by Ekaterina Kuskova, furthered the separation of liberal and social democratic (Marxist) methods of reform. The liberals favored trade unions, for instance, while the Marxists believed that professional revolutionaries should organize the workers to revolt against the government.

Kuskova's work urged reformers to follow the path that seemed most suited for Russia: Since the tsar had cut off all political action, Russian workers should form trade unions and strike for economic gain.[3]

This went totally against Lenin's belief in revolution. He worried so much about this attitude during his last months in Siberia that he lost weight and sleep.[4] By the time he left Siberia, he had engineered a meeting with seventeen exiles, and smuggled out a document called "The Protest by the Russian Social Democrats."[5]

Plekhanov and *Iskra*

Lenin planned to go to Switzerland to meet once again with Plekhanov, his hero, and begin implementing his plans for *Iskra*. He had no trouble obtaining a visa, but before leaving the country, he visited his wife, who was ill, and his mother in Moscow. He also made more revolutionary contacts in the provinces. He even took the chance of returning to St. Petersburg. With Yuli Martov, Lenin was caught by the police carrying two thousand rubles (Russian currency)—startup money for his newspaper. Miraculously, he was released and the money was not confiscated.

Lenin and another revolutionary named Alexander Potresov left immediately for Switzerland. Once there, things did not go so smoothly.

Lenin had a very forceful personality. He had emerged as the leader of the militant wing of Marxists within Russia. Plekhanov, on the other hand, was the undisputed revolutionary leader in exile. Plekhanov was critical of Lenin's writing style, and it was clear that he had no plan to give up his role as leader of the revolution to Lenin. He intended to be *Iskra*'s major contributor of ideas.[6]

Lenin published the first issue of *Iskra* in Leipzig, Germany, in 1900.

Lenin was disillusioned, but he was not about to give up control of anything. It was at this point that he stopped using pseudonyms—pen names—for his writing. The name V. I. Lenin, which may have come from the name of the River Lena in Siberia, became his fixed public identity.[7]

Although Plekhanov was granted two votes on decisions for the newspaper instead of the one vote each of the other five *Iskra* editors had, Lenin managed to get around this by having the newspaper printed in Germany instead of Switzerland. Plekhanov, in Switzerland, could only vote by mail—and the paper had to get printed on schedule whether Plekhanov's votes arrived or not.

When Nadezhda Krupskaya left Siberia, Lenin made her the secretary of *Iskra*, placing even more control over the paper in his own hands. *Iskra*, printed regularly and smuggled by revolutionaries to groups within Russia who faithfully handed it out, brought Lenin solid recognition as a prominent leader in exile.

Funding the Revolution

How did the growing number of exiled Marxist revolutionaries manage to eat, pay their rent, and finance all their comings and goings in and out of Russia and other European cities? Historian Dmitri Volkogonov pointed out that "At the time of the revolution of 1917, Lenin . . . had spent all of two years in paid work."[8] That had been when Lenin was a lawyer in St. Petersburg. Strangely, the majority of the professional revolutionaries—champions of the working class—had never known what it was like to work for a living. If they had been employed, there would never have been enough time to do all the writing, running back and forth, and agitating that preceded the Russian Revolution.

Lenin earned a small amount of money from the many pamphlets and articles he published in *Iskra* and elsewhere, but he was mainly supported until his mother's death by her pension and the sale of the family estate in Samara. Private benefactors also helped the revolutionary movement, including sympathizers such as the famous writer Maxim Gorky and other wealthy Russians. Increasingly, there were also party funds available, some of which came from "expropriations"—just plain stealing. A raid on two carriages filled with banknotes in Tbilisi, Georgia, the country south of Russia, killed three people and wounded many others. The robbery was carried out to obtain party funds. Since the banknotes were in large denominations, however, some of these were still uncashed by 1917, when the revolution

Primary Source—
Lenin's Declaration of the
Editorial Board of *Iskra*, 1900

In undertaking the publication of a political newspaper, *Iskra,* we consider it necessary to say a few words concerning the objects for which we are striving and the understanding we have of our tasks.

We are passing through an extremely important period in the history of the Russian working-class movement and Russian Social-Democracy. The past few years have been marked by an astonishingly rapid spread of Social-Democratic ideas among our intelligentsia, and meeting this trend in social ideas is an independent movement of the industrial proletariat, which is beginning to unite and struggle against its oppressors, and to strive eagerly towards socialism. The prisons and places of exile are filled to overflowing. Hardly a month goes by without our hearing of socialists "caught in dragnets" in all parts of Russia, of the capture of underground couriers, of the confiscation of literature and printing-presses. But the movement is growing, it is spreading to ever wider regions, it is penetrating more and more deeply into the working class and is attracting public attention to an ever-increasing degree. The entire economic development of Russia and the history of social thought and of the revolutionary movement in Russia serve as a guarantee that the Social-Democratic working-class movement will grow and will, in the end, surmount all the obstacles that confront it.[9]

began. All over Europe, revolutionaries were arrested when they tried to cash these notes.[10]

Most of the "expropriations," however, were of smaller sizes. Added to the donations from the ten thousand party members who lived in Russia after 1905, funding for revolutionary activity was never at risk. Lenin taught himself to handle money and keep books. He became accountant of all revolutionary funds.

A Divided Party

Between 1901 and 1905, the Marxist revolutionaries gained strength. But they also suffered a major split in ideologies.

The second congress (meeting) of the RSDLP was held in Brussels, Belgium, starting on July 30, 1903. To avoid police surveillance, it was then reopened in London on August 11 of that year. Although the congress was meant to help unite the revolutionaries, the result was instead a split into two different factions—the Bolsheviks and the Mensheviks.

Lenin headed the Bolsheviks, while the group headed mainly by Martov was called the Mensheviks. Though *Bolshevik* means "majority-ite," or the majority group, and Menshevik means "minority-ite," or minority group, the Mensheviks were actually in the majority at the second party congress.

The Mensheviks were the more moderate wing of the party. They believed that violence as a weapon for social change could be avoided through democracy, a parliament (legislature), and more than one political party. They also disagreed with the Bolshevik's "expropriations." Their ultimate goal was democracy.

The Bolsheviks, on the other hand, while still giving lip service in some of their writings to democracy, used it

Lenin, seen here in 1905, disagreed with the revolutionaries who believed that Russia should become a democracy.

as no more than a political show. Lenin and his followers believed in the value of violence. They equated social democracy with reform and Marxism with power. The dictatorship of the proletariat—carried out by a small, elite group of professional revolutionaries who hoped for world revolution—justified any means needed to bring it about. The Bolsheviks envisioned a nationless, classless world, with Russia as only one part.

A Call to Arms

These differences among the revolutionary factions were covered up by endless talk about organization. Who should join the party? What level of dedication—particularly to violent overthrow—was mandatory? Should there be a special combat organization?

When the third party congress was held in London in the spring of 1905, Lenin would give an impassioned speech about the need for armed violence. He tried to convince the congress that revolution was just around the corner. In his view, it was the Mensheviks, with their desire for peaceful change, who were getting in the way. Conciliation with any reform movement, including the Mensheviks, was against the Marxist cause and must be stopped. Meanwhile, back in Russia, where economic and social deprivation continued, more people were growing ready to heed Lenin's call to arms.

CHAPTER 7

The Road to Revolution

Despite the combative split between the Bolsheviks and the Mensheviks in the party, Russia's people were tired of living under the tsar. Workers began striking more often and students all over the country organized protests. A turning point on the road to revolution occurred as all social classes, including peasants and wealthier professionals, banded together to demand reforms and a representative government.

The Russo-Japanese War

In 1904, Russia went to war against Japan. At issue was control over Chinese territory in Manchuria. This war, six thousand miles from the Russian capital of St. Petersburg, meant that soldiers had to be mobilized and huge expenses had to be devoted to buying arms and supplying the troops.

It is important to understand the background behind this ill-advised war. Sergei Witte, a skilled diplomat who had been an advisor to two tsars, urged Tsar Alexander III to create funds to build a railway across Siberia. This Trans-

Siberian Railway, 5,876 miles long, was begun in 1891 and would be completed in 1916. As work neared completion on the final eastern segment, the Russians asked China for permission to run tracks through Chinese Manchuria to shorten the trip from Lake Baikal in southeastern Russia to the port at Vladivostok on the Pacific coast. China granted permission, but made it clear that the only Russian presence in Mongolia should be the railroad and its employees.[1]

By the time these negotiations took place with China, Nicholas II had become tsar. Under his leadership, Russia immediately broke its agreement and introduced police and military units to Mongolia. In fact, Russia made plans to annex—take over as its own territory—Chinese Manchuria. Problems arose because Japan, too, wished to take over the area.

In February 1904, with no warning, Japan attacked a naval base that Russia had leased from the Chinese at Port Arthur in Manchuria. The Japanese laid siege to the base, sank a great many ships, and took control of the China Sea. At first, the Russian people rallied to help the war effort. As the war dragged on, however, opinions changed dramatically.

Trouble at Home and Surrender

Because the war was going on thousands of miles away from St. Petersburg, troops made up of peasants and workers had to travel a great distance at great expense to fight the Japanese. Political unrest grew in opposition to the war—and the government. The hated minister of the interior, Vyacheslav Plehve, a master at police espionage, was assassinated. As it became apparent that Russia was losing the war, social democratic and liberal groups went into action to demonstrate their opposition to the government

Tsar Nicholas II ruled during one of the most volatile and unstable times in Russian history.

and the war. In December 1904, the Russians at Port Arthur surrendered. The Japanese captured whatever they had not already destroyed of Russia's Pacific fleet and took twenty-five thousand prisoners.

Father Grapon and Bloody Sunday

For several years before the war, a priest named Father Georgi Gapon had been busy establishing trade unions in St. Petersburg. At first, he had been persuaded to do this by the police, who thought unions they helped set up would avoid strikes and control the activities of the labor movement. Over time, however, Father Gapon came to identify with the grievances of the workers, and began to take their side in conflicts with government authorities—who had hired him in the first place.[2]

In January 1905, thousands of workers who had been dismissed from a large industrial plant held a protest march. Although most workers were still loyal to the tsar, they did want to gain more representation for their needs in the government. Father Gapon helped the workers organize a peaceful demonstration. He received permission from the police to hold the march, as long as the protesters did not get too close to the Winter Palace, one of the tsar's homes. Gapon did not know that Nicholas, to whom the workers were appealing for fair treatment, had left St. Petersburg the night before. On Sunday morning, January 22, a quiet procession of workers holding religious symbols called icons carried a petition to their tsar. As the procession got close to the palace, armed troops met it and told its members to leave. When the marchers did not obey immediately, the panicked troops fired on the crowd, killing two hundred people and wounding eight hundred others.[3]

Shock and outrage in response to the incident—called "Bloody Sunday"—reached all over the world.[4] Now all organizations—liberal and moderate, social democrats and socialist revolutionaries—protested the violence and condemned the government. Although there had been a history of workers' strikes in Russia since the 1870s, the Bloody Sunday demonstration marked the first time workers so forcefully appealed to the government for dramatic changes. After the bloodshed, hundreds of thousands of other workers went on strike, blaming the government for the outrageously violent incident.

After Defeat

Tsar Nicholas II, an often indecisive leader, took some measures to try to get the situation back under control. One of these measures was to declare the universities exempt from police surveillance and interference. All this did was open up the universities for the many radical groups, which were beginning to feel left out of the mass protests, and allow them to continue to agitate. Liberals, meanwhile, founded a group they called the Union of Unions. Many professional associations joined. It called for a constitutional monarchy to replace the tsar's autocracy (a government in which one person holds total power).

By May 1905, Japan had completed the humiliation of Russia by sinking the Russian ships that had tried to come to the rescue of the fleet the Japanese had already sunk earlier in the war. United States President Theodore Roosevelt stepped in and offered to act as an intermediary between Russia and Japan. Diplomat Sergei Witte went to meet with Japanese representatives in Portsmouth, New Hampshire, in the United States. Witte was able to negotiate terms that

On Bloody Sunday, hundreds of unarmed protestors were gunned down by Russian soldiers. This horrific event caused public outrage and strikes all across the region.

were far better than Russia could have expected. Russia was able to keep far eastern lands of the empire, with the exception of the Liaodong peninsula, the South Manchurian Railway, and the southern half of Sakhalin Island. Despite having been humiliated terribly in the war, Russia would remain a powerful nation on the Pacific, to the dismay of Japan. Although he was pleased with the good peace terms he had won, Witte returned home to a Russian Empire that was in disarray.

Tsar Nicholas' Choice

A national strike of essential services, including the railroad that was needed to bring Russian troops home from the east, was called. In October, the Union of Unions got strike committees ready to bring the country literally to a halt.

Tsar Nicholas called in Sergei Witte, who told the tsar there were two options: Nicholas could either declare the country a military dictatorship, or he could grant major political concessions to the disgruntled people. Witte knew that the first option was impossible. The army was six thousand miles away, and the railroads were not running. However, he knew he had to offer that option to Nicholas because it was the option the tsar would have preferred to implement, if it had been practical.[5] The other option— granting major changes—was the only real choice. Witte believed that if Nicholas could take charge of reforms and create a constitution, the appeal of the revolutionary factions would weaken. Witte stated in a prophetic memorandum:

> The advance of human progress is unstoppable. The idea of human freedom will triumph, if not by way of reform, then by way of revolution. But in the latter event it will come to life on the ashes of a thousand years of destroyed history. The Russian rebellion, mindless and pitiless, will sweep away everything, turn everything to dust. What kind of Russia will emerge from this unexampled trial transcends human imagination: the horrors of the Russian rebellion may surpass everything known to history. . . Attempts to put into practice the ideals of theoretical socialism—they will fail but they will be made, no doubt about it—will destroy the family, the expressions of religious faith, property, all the foundations of law.[6]

US President Theodore Roosevelt helped Sergei Witte negotiate an end to Russia's war with Japan in 1905. From left to right: Witte; Friedrich Rosen, Russian ambassador to the United States; Roosevelt; and Japanese negotiators D. Komura and K. Takahira.

Despite Witte's warning, Nicholas did not act. He held conferences with everyone he thought might be able to give him advice. His cousin Grand Duke Nikolai Nikolaevich told him that a military dictatorship was impossible. He also said that if Nicholas did not grant political liberties to Russia, he would shoot himself.[7]

The End of Autocracy in Russia

Once again, Witte stepped in. He drafted a manifesto (statement) that guaranteed civil rights for the Russian people and an elected legislature to be called the Duma. Finally, on October 30, Tsar Nicholas II, making sure the document did not contain the word constitution, signed the October Manifesto.

The signing of the October Manifesto effectively ended autocracy in Russia, but it did not solve Russia's problems. In fact, in the months after these political changes, excesses of all kinds occurred. Conservative Russians, who were loyal to the tsar and did not want to see the autocracy end, carried out pogroms—killing sprees that often wiped out whole villages—against Jews, simply because many social revolutionaries were Jewish. The peasants, confused by this mayhem, decided that they had license to seize private property from landowners. No one stepped in to stop this chaos. The new legislative process had not yet been implemented, and Tsar Nicholas was in no hurry to do anything about it.

The tsar was acting as if the revolution had never occurred. This attitude made the Duma, even after it began sessions, ineffective. Conservatives became more conservative and radical revolutionaries more radical during the first ten years in which the new political institutions were supposed to be in place.

Primary Source—From the October Manifesto, 1905

The disturbances and unrest in St. Petersburg, Moscow and in many other parts of our Empire ... could give rise to national instability and present a threat to the unity of Our State. The oath which We took as Tsar compels Us to use all Our strength, intelligence and power to put a speedy end to this unrest which is so dangerous for the State. . . . [I]n view of the need to speedily implement earlier measures to pacify the country, we have decided that the work of the government must be unified. We have therefore ordered the government to take the following measures . . . : 1. Fundamental civil freedoms will be granted to the population, including real personal inviolability, freedom of conscience, speech, assembly and association. 2. Participation in the Duma will be granted to those classes of the population which are at present deprived of voting powers. . . . 3. It is established as an unshakeable rule that no law can come into force without its approval by the State Duma and representatives of the people will be given the opportunity to take real part in the supervision of the legality of government bodies. We call on all true sons of Russia to remember the homeland, to help put a stop to this unprecedented unrest and, together with this, to devote all their strength to the restoration of peace to their native land.[8]

CHAPTER 8

Stunted Reforms

While the revolutionaries knew that the October Manifesto was not enough to change Russia for the better, they understood that it was an important step towards revolution. They continued to work hard to further their cause. The Bolsheviks organized to distribute Marxist revolutionary literature to Russian prisoners of war. The Mensheviks continued to work for practical solutions to the current crisis in Russia, although they came up with no ready answers.[1]

The only cooperation that occurred between the many small revolutionary factions took place during the pre-Manifesto period. Each crisis that arose was used as an opportunity to keep Russian workers thinking in a revolutionary way.[2]

Chief among those who made use of social unrest to promote revolution was a group called the St. Petersburg Soviet of Workers' Deputies. Through this group, Leon Trotsky, a social democrat who refused to ally himself with either Bolshevik or Menshevik factions, came to fame as a revolutionary. Trotsky was an excellent speaker who had strong appeal to large numbers of people.[3]

Shortly after the October Manifesto was signed, Trotsky was arrested and condemned to lifelong exile in the farthest reaches of Siberia. Just before reaching his final destination, he escaped. Wearing two fur coats and two pairs of boots, Trotsky made his way back across the snows of Siberia. Trotsky ended up in Finland. He attempted to be a conciliator between the Bolshevik and Menshevik factions.[4] The Mensheviks believed in pushing for action that would arise spontaneously from a large power base, including the masses of Russian people. The Bolsheviks, under Lenin's leadership, believed that a mass movement could only be brought about and controlled by a small, chosen, dedicated elite of professional revolutionaries.[5]

A Bolshevik Congress

In exile, the RSDLP continued to feud within itself along organizational and ideological lines. Lenin decided to leave *Iskra* and start an entirely new Bolshevik paper, which he called *Vpered* (Forward). *Iskra*, now under the more egalitarian leadership of Yuli Martov, a Menshevik and Lenin's former close colleague, became a forum for debate. It was no longer the beacon of revolutionary leadership Lenin had hoped it would be.

The RSDLP called a third party congress. It was held in London in April 1905. This congress was supposed to work toward reconciliation between Bolsheviks and Mensheviks. Instead, it became a Bolshevik congress when most Mensheviks, led by Plekhanov and Martov, refused to attend. This left Lenin poised to be the dominant leader of his party.[6] During the congress, he worked to organize his fellow Bolsheviks and to make the party ready for revolution—when the opportunity arrived.

Representatives of the Duma, the Russian legislature, at work in 1907.

After the October Manifesto

Lenin left for St. Petersburg shortly after the October Manifesto was issued. He arrived in November 1905. The country was in turmoil. All reformist organizations were both reveling in changes and pushing for more change with a united voice. Lenin, however, considered himself a leader. He would not join a faction to work from within. He contented himself with spreading the goal of eventual revolution, living in disguise and moving frequently to escape the police.

Primary Source—
V.I. Lenin's "Lessons of the
Moscow Uprising," 1906

In calling the strike, all the revolutionary parties, all the Moscow unions recognised and even intuitively felt that it must inevitably grow into an uprising. . . . From a strike and demonstrations to isolated barricades. From isolated barricades to the mass erection of barricades and street fighting against the troops. Over the heads of the organisations, the mass proletarian struggle developed from a strike to an uprising. This is the greatest historic gain the Russian revolution achieved in . . . 1905; and like all preceding gains it was purchased at the price of enormous sacrifices. The movement was raised from a general political strike to a higher stage. It compelled the reaction to go to the limit in its resistance, and so brought vastly nearer the moment when the revolution will also go to the limit in applying the means of attack. The reaction cannot go further than the shelling of barricades, buildings and crowds. But the revolution can go very much further than the Moscow volunteer fighting units, it can go very, very much further in breadth and depth. And the revolution has advanced far since December. The base of the revolutionary crisis has become immeasurably broader the blade must now be sharpened to a keener edge. . . As is always the case, practice marched ahead of theory, A peaceful strike and demonstrations immediately ceased to satisfy the workers; they asked: What is to be done next?[7]

Over the next months, however, he softened his position. Lenin encouraged Bolsheviks to try to take part in the government, starting with the Duma elections. He argued that this new legislature would be a perfect place to spread information about the RSDLP. He even advocated a reunion with the Mensheviks.[8]

Despite these views (and a fourth party congress in 1906), the period after the October Manifesto saw increasing conflict between the two branches of the party. Over time, Lenin's views would again become radical, but for the moment, he wanted to increase the party's strength in any way possible.

Party membership, which was at its peak at the time of the fifth party congress in the spring of 1907, began to dwindle. After the congress, Lenin did not return to Russia, for fear of capture. It would be almost ten years before he returned.

Undermining the October Manifesto

It looked as if Lenin's power, along with his exile, might continue without his ever seeing the revolution. Although terrorist activity still went on in Russia, it, too, dwindled as the government became stronger. With each year's new Duma elections, there were fewer socialists and liberals and more conservative and propertied members, which pleased the tsar. Even those revolutionary members who did remain seemed to be part of a shaky institution. In both 1906 and 1907, Tsar Nicholas II dismissed the Duma when he deemed it too radical. Not until the third Duma, beginning in November 1907, did the legislature serve a full term without the tsar's interference.

Sergei Witte managed to bring in foreign loans and draft a constitution for Russia. He began to implement the civil liberties promised by the October Manifesto, but then was himself suspected by the government of gaining too much power. He was dismissed. The tsar and his advisors further limited the powers of the Duma and the liberties granted by the October Manifesto. Then Pëtr A. Stolypin, Minister of the Interior, came on the scene.

Stolypin's Reforms

Stolypin was an even more skilled politician than Witte. He acted quickly to suppress acts of terrorism, executing those people suspected of rebellion. He also worked to secure foreign loans and to take steps toward agrarian—land use— reform. He presented the Duma with a law that allowed peasant families to withdraw from the communes, the social and land use system the government had decreed for the peasants, and apply for ownership of the land they had been allotted. This measure was not totally popular. The peasants had grown used to the security offered by communal land. By 1917, only 10 percent of eligible peasant households had chosen to become independent of the commune.

Wealthy landowners did not like this new law, either. They wanted to be the dominant force in rural Russia. Stolypin ran into problems from all factions as he tried to introduce bills that would actually make the Duma a partner in governing Russia. The tsar's government rebuffed his efforts because it had not wanted to end the autocracy in the first place. Liberals and socialists, on the other hand, worried that Stolypin's reforms would be successful, and that the revolution would be diluted and eventually buried. An assassin's bullet ended Stolypin's life in 1911.

Pëtr Stolypin, chairman of the Council of Ministers, faced a great deal of opposition when he tried to reform Russia's land use policies.

While the next three years seemed relatively peaceful in Russia, anxiety lay just beneath the surface. There was still no agreement among conflicting political factions. Hatred between ethnic groups and social classes was held in uneasy check only by the presence of the army and police. This delicate balance would not last long. Russia would soon be at war once again—both from within and from without.

Primary Source—From the Stolypin Land Reform, 1906

By our Manifesto of 3 November 1905, the levying on the peasantry of redemption payments for allotment land is abolished from 1 January 1907. From this time such lands are exempted from the restrictions placed on them as a result of the redemption debt and peasants receive the right freely to exit the Land Commune and to acquire as individual householders the rights of personal ownership of holdings from the Land Commune's allocation[9]

CHAPTER 9

The Great War

The years following the October Manifesto were very disappointing for Lenin. After the initial hope of true reform, the split in his party as well as the tsar's decision to limit the power of the Duma meant that not much had changed for the better in Russia. While in exile, Lenin and his wife moved frequently throughout Europe, spending long periods of time in Paris before settling in Switzerland. Lenin faced estrangement from the Mensheviks and even from the Bolsheviks for his belief that revolution was the only answer.

Two loyal followers stayed with him. Grigori Zinoviev and Lev Kamenev started a new revolutionary newspaper. It would become Lenin's main vehicle for furthering the Bolshevik cause. *Zvezda* (*The Star*), as the paper was called, was distributed secretly in St. Petersburg.

In April 1912, Russian government troops killed hundreds of striking mine workers, causing more strikes and violent reaction. The RSDLP was able to organize a legal worker newspaper, called *Pravda* (*Truth*), using Bolshevik funds. The paper, based in St. Petersburg, was very successful, but it only got Lenin into more trouble with the Mensheviks because it so clearly put forth his Bolshevik ideas.

Nicholas and Rasputin's Influence

Tsar Nicholas II made many mistakes during the years before the Russian Revolution. An indecisive man, he could not see beyond the traditional autocracy Russia had had for centuries. Forced by circumstances to sign the October Manifesto in 1905, he and his regime did their best to undermine any real liberty being offered to the Russian people. And yet, because of the customary adoration the peasant masses had for the role of the tsar, the end of the autocracy was not welcomed by the majority of the people it was meant to help.

Not only was Nicholas indecisive, but he was married to a woman who always urged him to make decisions in terms of autocracy. Empress Alexandra, who had been born a wealthy German princess and a granddaughter of England's Queen Victoria, came under the influence of a mystic named Rasputin. A monk with astounding powers of persuasion, Rasputin was able to cast hypnotic spells that helped Alexis, the tsar's son, who was a hemophiliac—someone whose blood does not clot normally and bleeds excessively when injured. The young prince seemed to benefit from Rasputin's treatments for his painful and life-threatening disease. Empress Alexandra was so grateful for Rasputin's help in easing her son's suffering that he became her advisor in all matters, even politics, though she chose to take his advice only when it suited her. Rasputin advised the tsar and his wife against entering World War I.[1]

Entering the War

World War I broke out in 1914 after Archduke Franz Ferdinand of Austria-Hungary was assassinated by a Serbian nationalist. The nations of Europe quickly took sides: Germany and Austria-Hungary formed the Central Powers with their allies, while Serbia, Great Britain, France, Russia, and other nations formed the Allied Powers.

Of all the mistakes Nicholas II made, becoming involved in World War I was perhaps his worst. At first, the war brought out national loyalties, inspiring some cooperation among the various factions and classes, and drawing attention away from internal unrest. Spirits were high when Russia mounted a successful offensive in Prussia (a German state, now part of Russia, Lithuania, Poland, and Germany) against Germany, and in Carpathia (located in the region of the Carpathian Mountains on the border between Belorussia and Poland) against Austrian-Hungarian troops. But this enthusiasm for the war did not last for long.

In the fall of 1914, at the Battle of Tannenberg in Germany, an attacking Russian army was left without backup forces. Two entire Russian corps, trapped in the woods, surrendered. Then, in the Battle of Masurian Lakes, a retreating German army routed the Russians, who lost one hundred twenty thousand men. By the time the two battles were over, the Russian Army had lost two hundred fifty thousand men—a quarter of its troops. Because of poorly maintained railroads, the rest of the Russian Army in Germany ran out of weapons and then out of food. The Russian Army was starving to death and vulnerable to attack. The soldiers lived in chaos, lashing out at each other and their superiors.

On the advice of his wife and Rasputin, Tsar Nicholas decided to fire the head Russian Army com-mander, his uncle the Grand Duke Nikolai Nikolaevich. Nicholas himself would become Commander in Chief of the armed forces. He would devote himself full-time to fighting the war. Although his presence stabilized the worst of the anarchy in the army, Nicholas left Russia to be run by Empress Alexandra and Rasputin. During his absence, strikes happened regularly, food became scarce to the point of famine, and inflation and corruption were everywhere. Still, the tsar refused to step in and change decisions that were made by his wife.

Grigori Rasputin, a peasant and a mystic, became a trusted and influential friend of Tsar Nicholas II and his family. Many believe that he contributed to the growing unpopularity of the royal family.

Finally, the entire country seemed to have had enough of this ineffective tsar. In late 1916, angry members of the nobility assassinated Rasputin, hoping the government would be better without his influence. Even that move, however, came too late. "The regime proved incapable of governing in a critical situation," according to historian Dmitri Volkogonov.[2] A major revolution was about to occur—but where were its leaders?

Revolutionary Leaders' Response to War

Socialists from all of the countries participating in World War I were divided into three camps: Defensists basically felt they should hold off on revolutionary activity and help their native country fight the war. Internationalists disagreed, believing that workers—no matter what country they came from—should not be killing each other to make the capitalist system stronger. Defeatists hoped their own country would lose the war, because they believed a defeat would weaken the government that the socialists were working to destroy.

Lenin believed in both of the latter two positions. He saw the war as an excellent opportunity to further the Marxist revolution. Because he was living in Austrian Poland at the time, which was at war with Russia, he was arrested in the early days of the war by the Austrian police. However, he was able to convince the authorities that he wanted nothing to do with Russia's war effort. He was allowed to move to Switzerland with his wife.

There, he went to the libraries, took long walks, and continued his writing. Lenin's financial condition grew worse, partly because of the death of his mother, who had helped support him through all the years of his exile.

Because of the war, communications to and from Russia were difficult. The Germans, however, saw in Lenin a chance to further their own efforts. In conversations with Lenin, German officials took in the major messages of his revolutionary writing. It was the Germans, not the Bolsheviks, who flooded the Russian war trenches with revolutionary propaganda.

Despite the unrest in Russia, the army's terrible situation, and the shift in public mood about the tsar, only parts of

A group of wounded Russian prisoners of war march to a German hospital in 1916. Both the Russian military as well as the Russian people suffered tremendous losses during World War I.

this nationwide despair filtered out of Russia to the isolated exiles. In early 1917, the forty-seven-year-old Lenin gave a speech celebrating the 1905 revolution, which he had hoped would be a prelude to a future Marxist revolution. He recognized, however, that this second revolution seemed to be a long way off. To a small audience, he said, "We old folks may not live to see the decisive battles of the coming revolution."[3] He was wrong.

Primary Source—
V.I. Lenin's "Lecture on the 1905 Revolution," 1917

We must not be deceived by the present grave-like stillness in Europe. Europe is pregnant with revolution. The monstrous horrors of the imperialist war, the suffering caused by the high cost of living everywhere engender a revolutionary mood; and the ruling classes, the bourgeoisie, and its servitors, the governments, are more and more moving into a blind alley from which they can never extricate themselves without tremendous upheavals.

Just as in Russia in 1905, a popular uprising against the tsarist government began under the leadership of the proletariat with the aim of achieving a democratic republic, so, in Europe, the coming years, precisely because of this predatory war, will lead to popular uprisings under the leadership of the proletariat against the power of finance capital, against the big banks, against the capitalists; and these upheavals cannot end otherwise than with the expropriation of the bourgeoisie, with the victory of socialism.

We of the older generation may not live to see the decisive battles of this coming revolution. But I can, I believe, express the confident hope that the youth which is working so splendidly in the socialist movement of Switzerland, and of the whole world, will be fortunate enough not only to fight, but also to win, in the coming proletarian revolution.[4]

CHAPTER 10

The February Revolution

By 1917, both Russian civilians and soldiers were tired of the war. Close to five million Russian men were captured or lost their lives, and the Russian army was often in retreat. The economy also suffered due to the war. The price of food increased drastically. Even if a family could afford to buy the food they needed, shops often closed because they did not have enough bread, sugar, or meat to sell. Factories were forced to close because of fuel shortages, and families lined up in front of bakeries for free bread. By February Russian workers had begun organized strikes. For the first time, the troops that were called in by the tsar to stop the strikers could not do so. Many officers sympathized with the strikers and were disgusted with both the war and the tsar.

On March 8, crowds milled about on the main avenue of Petrograd. The Russian capital had been renamed at the start of the war because Russians believed "St. Petersburg" sounded too German. People held up signs saying, "Down with the Autocracy" and "Down with the War."[1] Those who stood in the breadlines soon broke up and joined the rioting crowd. Looting began. City services soon came to a halt.

Russian workers strike in Petrograd in 1917. Demonstrations like these marked the beginning of the February Revolution.

Social Unrest and Rioting

The tsar's ministers realized that something drastic had to be done. There had never been such mass disruption in Russia. They sent word to the tsar, who was in far-off Mogilev in the south of Russia, monitoring the war effort and caring for his children, who had measles. As usual, Nicholas II underestimated the problems and what had to be done to solve them. He sent word to Petrograd that force must be used to stop the rioting. Within a few days, enough troops had been gathered to make the city appear calm.

On March 10, however, a regiment of soldiers fired on a group of protesters when they refused to leave. Forty civilians were killed or wounded. This incident, in turn, caused a mutiny in a garrison that was composed of men who had been recruited past the usual draft age because all the young men were already at the war front. These men—one hundred sixty thousand of them were cooped up in barracks that usually accommodated twenty thousand—were in no mood to shoot their fellow Russians in order to defend a government they now hated. The men refused to obey future orders to shoot at civilians, and many other regiments followed suit.

On March 11, a crowd invaded the city's Litovski Prison and burned it down.[2] Rioters also raided the Ministry of the Interior, stole weapons from military arsenals, and hung a red flag (red was a Communist symbol) over the tsar's Winter Palace. The few remaining loyal troops shot rioters and demonstrators, but Petrograd was clearly being run by peasants, who were, by now, in uniform.

The Duma Committee

The Duma, ignoring Nicholas's recent orders to dissolve, met. Its members had no idea what to do, but it realized it was the only alternative to the tsar and that it had to do something.[3] Thousands of people—soldiers, peasants, and workers—were marching to Taurida Palace where the Duma met, proclaiming allegiance to a body of legislators that was itself confused and divided politically.

On March 12, the Duma rallied, however, and agreed to establish a new government and a whole new social order for Russia. It would form a Provisional Government, to be headed by Mikhail Rodzianko, the Duma chairman. This was done in the absence of any revolutionary leaders, who on the same day formed the Petrograd Soviet, a representative governmental body that would rival the Duma for power. This act was initiated mainly by the Mensheviks. The Soviet represented workers and soldiers. Out of three thousand deputies, "more than 2000 were soldiers—this in a city that had two or three times as many industrial workers as servicemen. These figures illustrate the extent to which the February Revolution in its initial phase was a soldier mutiny."[4]

There were many people in the Soviet, all of whom had the right to make long speeches. This meant that no decisions would be made at the first meetings of the Petrograd Soviet. An executive committee was formed, the Ispolkom. It acted to unify and organize socialist groups, under the name of the full Soviet. Unlike the Duma, the Ispolkom worked to further, rather than end, the revolution.[5]

The Ispolkom

Although the Provisional Government held the official leadership role between March and November 1917, the government was in fact run by the Ispolkom. By immediately dissolving the police and calling for nationwide elections for self-government, the Ispolkom canceled all provincial bureaucracy—offices that ran the countryside: "They abolished in one fell swoop the entire administrative and security structure that had kept the Russian state intact for a century or more," wrote historian Richard Pipes.[6] Another disastrous mistake was that the government was given no real authority over the armed and angry peasant soldiers.

Alexander Kerensky, a lawyer from Simbirsk, was a leader in the Provisional Government following the overthrow of Tsar Nicholas II in 1917.

The most important leader to emerge from this chaos was Alexander Kerensky, a thirty-six-year-old lawyer. He was, interestingly, the son of the Alexander Kerensky who, as a school director, had recommended young Vladimir Lenin for college. The younger Kerensky was an excellent, emotional speaker, energetic and vain. He had risen to political power by representing striking gold miners in 1905. He was a moderate socialist, a believer in labor causes who was able to win the loyalty of workers, soldiers, moderate socialists, and even some of the radical socialists. He proclaimed from balconies that Russia's suffering was over, and that there would soon be world peace. He was the one leader who was a member of both the Provisional Government and the Ispolkom—for which Lenin would never forgive him.

The Tsar Steps Down

Tsar Nicholas II, who still could not believe that he had actually lost power, was approaching Petrograd in his train as the city fell to the new Provisional Government. On the train, he considered proclaiming Russia a constitutional monarchy. These thoughts, however, came years too late. Perhaps, had Nicholas been able to make peace quickly with Germany and bring back the troops to help regain the city, the revolution might have been contained. Though he considered this, Nicholas became convinced that for the good of Russia, he would have to abdicate—give up his position as tsar of Russia.

Nicholas was met at his train by two members of the Provisional Government. They demanded that he step down from the throne. Nicholas abdicated, not in favor of his son, Alexis, whose hemophilia might cause his death before he reached adulthood, but instead Nicholas's younger brother

A sketch shows Tsar Nicholas II presenting his abdication in a railcar as he returns to Petrograd.

Michael. Grand Duke Michael, angered by this unwanted "privilege" and afraid for his life, refused to accept the throne. With his refusal, the Russian monarchy was dissolved.

Nicholas and his family were placed under house arrest at Tsarskoe Selo, one of their country homes near Petrograd. There, they would remain for five months while

Primary Source— Nicholas II's Declaration of Abdication, 1917

By the Grace of God, We, Nikolai II, Emperor of All the Russias, Tsar of Poland, Grand Duke of Finland, and so forth, to all our faithful subjects be it known: . . . In these decisive days in the life of Russia we have thought that we owed to our people the close union and organisation of all its forces for the realisation of a rapid victory; for which reason, in agreement with the Imperial Duma, we have recognized that it is for the good of the country that we should abdicate the Crown of the Russian State and lay down the Supreme Power.

Not wishing to separate ourselves from our beloved son, we bequeath our heritage to our brother, the Grand Duke Mikhail Alexandrovich, with our blessing for the future of the Throne of the Russian State. . . .

We call upon all faithful sons of our native land to fulfil their sacred and patriotic duty of obeying the Tsar at the painful moment of national trial and to aid them, together with the representatives of the nation, to conduct the Russian State in the way of prosperity and glory. May God help Russia.[7]

the Provisional Government tried to decide what should be done with them.

Return to Russia

Exiles from Siberia and from countries all over the world now began their trips home to Russia. One of the first to arrive was Joseph Stalin, who came originally from the southern Russian province of Georgia. Stalin was an active Bolshevik who had been an editor of *Pravda* before he was arrested and sent to Siberia. He and Lev Kamenev found themselves the most influential Bolsheviks present in Petrograd in March. They decided to explore compromise with the Provisional Government, so as to appear to be in tune with the mood of the masses.[8] Stalin also spoke of trying to find common ground with the Mensheviks and other revolutionary groups.

Leon Trotsky, who had been running a socialist newspaper in Brooklyn, New York, did not arrive in Petrograd until May. Though he was of great use to the party because of his intelligence and his incisive, charismatic, and inflammatory speeches, Trotsky had never been part of the main organizing body of Bolsheviks. Like Provisional Government leader Alexander Kerensky, Trotsky often allowed personal vanity to interfere with expressing his ideas to other people.

Lenin, on the other hand, had a firmness of purpose that did not waver. Even when his stance made him unpopular, he never appeared personally arrogant. However, Lenin had not yet reached Russia, and there was nothing he could do from afar to bring about compromise among the Bolsheviks. When he reached Russia on April 16, the revolution would take on a different face.

Primary Source— From Lenin's Speech to Soldiers, 1917

Comrade soldiers! The question of the state system is now on the order of the day. The capitalists, in whose hands the state power now rests, desire a parliamentary bourgeois republic, that is, a state system where there is no tsar, but where power remains in the hands of the capitalists who govern the country by means of the old institutions, namely: the police, the bureaucracy, and the standing army.

We desire a different republic, one more in keeping with the interests of the people, more democratic. The revolutionary workers and soldiers of Petrograd have overthrown tsarism, and have cleaned out all the police from the capital. The workers of all the world look with pride and hope to the revolutionary 'workers and soldiers of Russia as the vanguard of the world's liberating army of the working class. The revolution, once begun, must be strengthened and carried on. We shall not allow the police to be re-established! All power in the state, from the bottom up, from the remotest little village to every street block of Petrograd, must belong to the Soviets of Workers', Soldiers', Agricultural Labourers', Peasants' and other Deputies. The central state power uniting these local Soviets must be the Constituent Assembly, National Assembly, or Council of Soviets—no matter by what name you call it.[9]

CHAPTER 11

Lenin's Rise to Power

The train carrying Lenin pulled into Finland Station in Petrograd on April 16. After ten years of exile, Lenin had returned to Russia. Before arriving, Lenin had sent a message to friends in Petrograd that his arrival should not be seen as an ordinary return, but rather as the return of a leader.[1] Workers gathered at the station flew banners and uttered revolutionary slogans at Lenin's arrival. After exiting the train, Lenin was carried on workers' shoulders to an armored car that stood ready for him. Standing on top of the car, the formerly exiled leader spoke to his supporters.

In his speech, welcomed by many but shocking to others, Lenin declared his intent not to work with the Provisional Government.[2] He said it had done nothing but deceive the people. Lenin promised to continue, with the people, to fight for world revolution. Lenin was taken to Bolshevik headquarters, a lavish villa the party had taken over from a famous ballerina named M. F. Kshesinskaia, said in her youth to have been the tsar's mistress. At this time, although the Provisional Government was indecisive and the Petrograd Soviet still disorganized, the Bolsheviks had no more than

Lenin speaks to revolutionaries at the headquarters in Petrograd. After Lenin returned to Russia, he encouraged his followers to rise up and overthrow the Provisional Government.

two hundred thousand members and followers. The Russian population at that time was around 150 million. The outer reaches of the empire were only now, as the snows melted, beginning to hear that a revolution had occurred.

The Controversial "Theses"

The very next day, Lenin proposed the so-called "April Theses." This document "impressed most members of his audience as written by someone out of touch with reality, if not positively mad [insane]."[3] At first, *Pravda* refused to print the theses. When it did, the editors wrote an article saying that the theses were only Lenin's views, not their own. "They [the Bolsheviks] were being told by their leader to turn the Soviet into a battering ram, and with it to demolish the Provisional Government," according to historian Harold Shukman.[4] Gradually, the Bolsheviks accepted Lenin's views but "[i]t remained an open question whether Lenin's strategy was that of a master politician or simply that of a cranky extremist."[5]

Lenin's "Theses" called for World War I to stop at any cost, and for the revolution to continue to its next phase—there should be no stopping to allow the middle class to create a democracy. It was time, he said, to move directly to a Marxist, or Communist, state. He said the Provisional Government must be replaced, and a people's militia would replace the army. All land was to be seized in the name of the nation. All power must rest in the Soviets—the popular councils—including all industrial production and distribution. There would be a single national bank. He promised the people peace, bread, and land—welcome words to people who had only recently been on the verge of starvation. Over the next six months, the Bolsheviks' amazing rise to power would make it clear that the "Bolsheviks were bound together not by what they believed but in whom they believed [Lenin]."[6]

Lenin had no intention of merely taking over the existing government bodies. Instead, he would try to eliminate the old institutions entirely, replacing them with new government structures. Lenin would also avoid counterrevolutionary tactics (actions by those who wanted to stop the revolution) by eliminating the counterrevolutionaries—by whatever means necessary.

German Support

Germany was delighted that Lenin had taken a hard line on the war. Revolution and a world war were incompatible, and the Germans would be the ones to benefit most from Lenin's ardent antiwar stance. It is clear that German money helped, if not ensured, the Bolsheviks' rise to power. Some estimates put the total amount given by Germany to the Bolsheviks at somewhere between $6 million and $10 million, although this was kept highly secret after Lenin's return.

The Soviets Control the Provisional Government

After Lenin published the "April Theses," the next important Bolshevik move was the formation, in May, of the Bolshevik Red Guard, a militia that would grow larger over time. The Bolsheviks were good at organizing. When disagreements between the Provisional Government and the Soviet over ways to handle the war effort led to street demonstrations, the Bolsheviks were right there, spreading antigovernment slogans. They called for the Soviet to take over the government. Despite these forceful tactics on the part of the

Lenin delivers the "April Theses." In his remarks, he set forth his goals for establishing a Communist state.

Bolsheviks, General Lavr Kornilov was turned down by the Provisional Government when he asked to use force against the Bolshevik demonstrators.

The Provisional Government admitted that it was having little success in running the country. It offered the Bolsheviks positions in the cabinet (executive advisors), an offer they had formerly refused but now decided to accept. Next, the creation of a new coalition government played right into the hands of the Bolsheviks. Dual power—

Primary Source— V.I. Lenin's "The Tasks of the Proletariat in the Present Revolution," 1917

The specific feature of the present situation in Russia is that the country is passing from the first stage of the revolution—which, owing to the insufficient class-consciousness and organisation of the proletariat, placed power in the hands of the bourgeoisie—to its second stage, which must place power in the hands of the proletariat and the poorest sections of the peasants.

This transition is characterised, on the one hand, by a maximum of legally recognised rights (Russia is now the freest of all the belligerent countries in the world); on the other, by the absence of violence towards the masses, and, finally, by their unreasoning trust in the government of capitalists, those worst enemies of peace and socialism.

This peculiar situation demands of us an ability to adapt ourselves to the special conditions of Party work among unprecedentedly large masses of proletarians who have just awakened to political life.[7]

shared by the Provisional Government and the Soviets—had been troublesome. Now the Soviets would dominate the Provisional Government, yet remain an independent body.

As part of the government, however, the Soviets were blamed when things went wrong. Still, the Bolsheviks declared that they were the only alternative—the Soviets alone could save Russia. Since the Bolsheviks wanted world revolution, and did not necessarily feel loyal to Russia itself, historian Richard Pipes explained, "they could . . . act with complete irresponsibility, promising every group whatever it wanted and encouraging every destructive trend."[8] According to Sheila Fitzpatrick, it was the Bolshevik's "faith rather than scientific prediction that world revolution was imminent" that led them to pursue these policies in Russia.[9]

Antiwar propaganda was carried out quietly among the troops at the war front. Alexander Kerensky, now war minister, gave ringing speeches that rallied troops for hours after he left. But the soldiers were tired after three years—tired of suffering and tired of the mixed attitudes toward the war that were reaching them from Petrograd.

A Coup is Called Off

In June, the Bolsheviks planned a mass demonstration against the war, but they lacked the centrality of purpose to actually carry it out. The Russian Army had one more victory against Germany, led by General Kornilov, but was then quickly routed by Austrians coming to Germany's aid. For Russia, the war just fell apart. Russians soldiers fled for home.

Once again, the antiwar Bolsheviks organized street riots. Meanwhile, Lenin was in Finland, taking a break. He had been suffering from headaches and, according to a friend,

When the Provisional Government began arresting Bolsheviks, Lenin fled in disguise to Finland. In this photo he is almost unrecognizable without his trademark beard.

"his face was white and his eyes showed great fatigue."[10] His rest was cut short by the increasing anger at the continuation of the war. Workers and soldiers who did not want to go to the front presented a perfect opportunity for organization by the Bolsheviks. Lenin hurriedly returned to Petrograd.

Though Lenin later claimed that the demonstration he organized on July 17 was meant to be a peaceful means of taking power, it appears that he hoped the time for decisive action had finally come. However, since Lenin had come back to Russia only that morning, news of rioting, looting, pogroms, and general chaos made him lose "his nerve."[11] Perhaps there had not been enough organizing beforehand. Or perhaps, as historian Dmitri Volkogonov believed, "Having brought out half a million people, the Bolsheviks had acted without a clear plan or precise direction."[12] Whatever the reason, Lenin called off the planned coup (government overthrow).

The Provisional Government, frightened because it knew the armed Bolshevik troops could easily have taken over Taurida Palace, where it had its offices, released some information condemning the Bolsheviks for treason in dealings with the Germans. These accusations rallied government troops, who occupied the city, hunting for and arresting Bolsheviks the entire next week. Lenin, a master of disguises, first hid in various safe houses in Petrograd, and then, once again, fled as an exile to Finland.

CHAPTER 12

The October Revolution

Support for the Bolsheviks increased steadily as Russians grew tired of the war. By September 1917, Bolshevik membership skyrocketed. While Lenin's brief return certainly helped increase support, there were other capable leaders who reached out to the Russian population. Trotsky joined the Bolsheviks in July and was an excellent orator who used his speaking skills to earn the trust of many Russians. But General Kornilov, appointed Commander in Chief of the armed forced by Alexander Kerensky, helped the party more than anyone. Returning from the warfront angry and defeated, Kornilov stated he would only accept the post if certain military reforms were implemented. Kerensky agreed, but then delayed passing the reforms.

A former Provisional Government official who, up to that time, had been a minor player in revolutionary intrigue, emerged to unwittingly save the day for the Bolsheviks. Vladimir Lvov, in a complicated mix-up of messages between Kerensky and Kornilov, managed to convince both men that each was about to betray the other and make himself dictator. If the long-term results were not so tragic, the back-and-forth messages would have been comical. But what did result was that Kerensky, though he became aware that Kornilov had also been misled, relieved him of his command and charged him with treason. Kerensky then asked the Bolsheviks for their help. Forty thousand guns were given out to workers, to stave off Kornilov's supposed military takeover. The majority of these guns became the basic arsenal of the Bolshevik Red Guards.

Instead of increasing his authority within the government, however, the Kornilov affair cut off Kerensky from any future military help. Since it appeared that Kornilov, given his views on the ineffectiveness of the government, might have tried a takeover, the officers of the garrison would not get involved to help Kerensky. They felt that Kornilov had been treated unjustly. Kerensky's days as a leader were numbered.

Lenin Urges Action

Lenin and Grigori Zinoviev, disguised as farm laborers in Finland, kept up with the news from Russia through secret messengers. Though dispirited by the failure of the July demonstrations to turn into a complete overthrow of the government, Lenin kept up his writing. In addition to articles and letters, he worked on a book he had begun in Switzerland. It was called *State and Revolution*.

When he heard about the Kornilov-Kerensky mess in which Kerensky was actually helping to arm the Bolsheviks, Lenin's mood improved greatly.[1] By September, when Leon Trotsky became chairman of the Petrograd Soviet, Bolshevik power was on the upswing. Trotsky advocated using a nationwide organization of Soviets, in which Bolsheviks held power. This would be done for the sole purpose of seizing

91

Russian support for overthrowing the government continued to grow throughout 1917. Here a crowd gathers to receive revolutionary newspapers.

control of all the other Soviets, including that of Petrograd.[2] Again, the Bolsheviks were split over their readiness to bring this about.

By way of letter from Finland, Lenin urged, "The Bolsheviks can and must seize power."[3] Trotsky, too, was in favor of swift movement. Kamenev and Zinoviev voted against an overly quick move. They said it would risk the party, as well as the Russian and world revolutions.[4]

Lenin was infuriated. He saw anyone who opposed his revolutionary goals as an enemy. He wanted Kamenev and Zinoviev expelled from the party because of their dissenting opinion. In 1902, Lenin had proclaimed, "give us an organization of revolutionaries and we will overturn Russia."[5] Nothing had changed.

The rest of the party leadership, however, did not see the need or the sense of immediate action. Russia was still involved in World War I, though few soldiers remained at the front. The Provisional Government still had commitments to the Allies. A meeting, or congress, of the various Soviets was soon to take place. The Bolsheviks could use the Soviets to assume power peacefully.

Lenin exploded. In letters he asked: What if the government surrendered Petrograd to the Germans? What if the elections, scheduled by the government to be held on November 12, resulted in an actual democratic election of revolutionaries? How, then, could the Bolsheviks continue to act for the people—as Lenin believed they must—when the people had already elected for themselves?[6]

Once again, Lenin had to back down and wait. But the Bolsheviks did not waver or act confused—however confused they may have been. As anarchy in the country increased, the Petrograd Soviet did not try to prevent the Bolsheviks from having time to gather pro-Bolshevik delegates for the congress of Soviets. The congress quickly focused on gaining approval for a Bolshevik coup.

Fear of German Occupation

Germany had completed a naval operation that occupied three islands close to Petrograd. Russians now wondered if the capital should move to Moscow, which was farther inland. The Bolshevik Soviets did not want this, because it might help to strengthen the Provisional Government. When it was decided that the government would remain in Petrograd, the Bolsheviks offered their military services

Primary Source— V.I. Lenin's Call to Power, 1917

The situation is critical in the extreme. In fact it is now absolutely clear that to delay the uprising would be fatal. With all my might I urge comrades to realize that everything now hangs by a thread; that we are confronted by problems which are not to be solved by conferences or congresses (even congresses of Soviets), but exclusively by peoples, by the masses, by the struggle of the armed people. . . . We must not wait! We may lose everything! . . . History will not forgive revolutionaries for procrastinating when they could be victorious today (and they certainly will be victorious today), while they risk losing much tomorrow, in fact, they risk losing everything. If we seize power today, we seize it not in opposition to the Soviets but on their behalf. The seizure of power is the business of the uprising; its political purpose will become clear after the seizure. . . . The government is tottering. It must be given the death-blow at all costs.[7]

for the defense of the capital. As the only military unit not controlled by the Provisional Government, this would put the Bolsheviks in control.

By this time, Lenin had resurfaced in Petrograd. This was extremely dangerous for him, but he did not trust that other Bolsheviks would act swiftly, decisively, and at the correct time without his being there to help direct their actions.

Lenin wanted a coup to occur immediately. Kamenev and Zinoviev thought it should come later. Trotsky and some others believed that the coup should occur in conjunction with the congress of Soviets that would take place on November 7.

Lenin's strategy was offensive, but it claimed to be defensive, hiding behind the excuse that the Germans were about to take over, so the Bolsheviks had to save the day.[8] The Provisional Government, as usual, used half measures in its effort to contain the Bolsheviks, exposing its own lack of unity and decisiveness. Though the government shut down several Bolshevik newspapers, it failed to stop growing Bolshevik military strength. Given power by the government, the Bolsheviks, in the name of the Soviet, had formed a military-revolutionary committee called the Milrevkom. This committee controlled only a minority of Petrograd's troops in October. By early November, however, the Milrevkom had enlisted a large number of other military units by convincing soldiers that they must defend the revolution against a weak government that might give in to the Germans.

A Bloodless Coup

On the night of November 6–7, the Bolsheviks took over the city of Petrograd. Pickets were posted, and anyone who objected was disarmed. No violence occurred as the Milrevkom took over telephone and telegraph offices, banks, bridges, and railroad lines. Military staff headquarters became Bolshevik quarters. According to one participant, in the most casual manner imaginable, "They [the Bolsheviks] entered and sat down while those who had been sitting there got up and left; thus the Staff was taken."[9]

Alexander Kerensky tried to get military backup to protect the Provisional Government at the Winter Palace but failed. He fled toward the war front the next morning. However, the Winter Palace was not yet Bolshevik territory, and Lenin wanted it to be captured. The evening had gone so smoothly that no troops could be seen. The few Bolsheviks who were willing to assault the Winter Palace retreated when they heard shots.

Nevertheless, Lenin, at party headquarters, proclaimed victory for the revolution of workers, soldiers, and peasants. He drafted a declaration that recognized "sovereign power over Russia to have been assumed by a body that no one except the Bolshevik Central Committee had authorized to do so."[10] Because there was no violence and the night had been virtually undisturbed, on the morning of November 7, people went on with their lives as usual.

Kerensky, from the war front, tried to get the army to restore order to Petrograd. Other forces got close to Petrograd, fired a few ineffectual shots, and stopped. The governmental cabinet, trapped in the Winter Palace, sat around waiting for help. Outside defenders, tired of waiting for reinforcements, drifted away.

There were still government troops and ministers of the Provisional Government in the Winter Palace. All that day, small groups of Bolsheviks entered the palace. They let themselves be disarmed by the bedraggled government troops while trying to convince them to join the Bolshevik cause. By 2:00 a.m. on November 8, Red Guard and sailor troops were able to storm the Winter Palace without firing a shot. The Bolsheviks, with nobody trying to stop them, entered the Winter Palace and arrested the members of the cabinet. In the small room where the ministers waited, a

Bolsheviks storm the Winter Palace during the October Revolution. Incredibly, no shots were fired during the takeover.

revolutionary named Vladimir Antonov-Ovseenko declared, "In the name of the Military and Revolutionary Committee of the Petrograd Soviet, I declare the Provisional Government deposed. All are arrested."[11] The former ministers were taken as prisoners to Peter and Paul Fortess.

Lenin's declaration of successful revolution was approved by the congress of Soviets, which met until dawn. Not everyone was happy about the Bolsheviks' success. The more moderate revolutionary delegates left the meeting to show their disapproval.

So far, the revolution had occurred without bloodshed. If not a total surprise to both the revolutionaries themselves and to people of Petrograd, the revolution was at least unexpected in its scope and suddenness. It was so sudden, in fact, that few people thought it would last until the end of the year. Trotsky, writing later about the coup, said:

> If neither Lenin nor I had been present in Petersburg, there would have been no October Revolution [the coup took place in October rather than November on the old-style Russian calendar]: the leadership of the Bolshevik Party would have prevented it from occurring—of this I have not the slightest doubt! If Lenin had not been in Petersburg, I doubt whether I could have managed to conquer the resistance of the Bolshevik leaders.[12]

While there was some disagreement among the Bolsheviks, however, some historians have questioned whether the October revolution was simply a coup or if it was backed by popular support. According to historian

Lenin and Trotsky (right) in 1917. Trotsky credited Lenin and himself with successfully leading the October Revolution.

Orlando Figes, "The October insurrection was a coup d'état, actively supported by a small minority of the population, but it took place amidst a social revolution, which was centered on the popular realization of Soviet power."[13] Whether or not the Russian population supported this coup, the Bolsheviks would care little for the opinions of the masses once they attained power.

Primary Source— V.I. Lenin's Speech to the Citizens of Russia, 1917

The Provisional Government has been deposed. State power has passed into the hands of the organ of the Petrograd Soviet of Workers' and Soldiers' Deputies— the Revolutionary Military Committee, which heads the Petrograd proletariat and the garrison.

The cause for which the people have fought, namely, the immediate offer of a democratic peace, the abolition of landed proprietorship, workers' control over production, and the establishment of Soviet power—this cause has been secured.

Long live the revolution of workers, soldiers and peasants![14]

CHAPTER 13

The Bolsheviks Take Over

Lenin and the Bolsheviks had been dreaming of and planning for revolution for years. Now that the revolution had taken place, however, the time had come to govern this new state that was once the Russian Empire. While the Bolsheviks were skilled in revolutionary tactics, demonstrations, and political organizing, they had no experience in government administration. Could they successfully govern a population of 150 million Russians?

The Soviet of People's Commissars

Harold Shukman, a British philosopher, defined Bolshevism as "an impatient philosophy, which aims at creating a new world without sufficient preparation in the opinions and feelings of ordinary men and women."[1] It was the ordinary men, women, and children of Russia who would suffer to allow that ideology to succeed.

The first thing the new Bolshevik leaders had to do was stop any threat that Alexander Kerensky could come back to Petrograd with enough army troops to stage a countercoup.

Kerensky was able to gather only a small force before he once again escaped, and finally went to America. There, he wrote and lectured, living to the age of eighty.

With Kerensky gone, there remained the problem of governing. First, the Bolsheviks wanted new names for the members of the government. The old term ministers was considered too much of a reminder of the old tsarist regime. Members of the government would now be called People's Commissars.[2] The government itself would be called the Soviet of People's Commissars. This suggestion was Trotsky's. Lenin liked it because it sounded revolutionary.[3]

Lenin was now the manager of this new government, which proposed to rule over 150 million Russians of varied class and ethnic backgrounds. As he led seemingly endless meetings, Lenin insisted that members of the *Sovnarkom*, the party cabinet, be on time and stick exactly to the time allotted for their speeches. Being tardy or absent resulted in punishment. Lenin himself worked constantly, as usual, but the tediousness of running a government was difficult for a man who, for years, had moved around from country to country, never having to follow a daily routine. He became continually tired.

Lenin worked to make sure state and local organizations were always under the tight control of the centralized government. According to historian Dmitri Volkogonov, "The old state machine had been broken and the new one was primitive, inefficient and from its very inception markedly bureaucratic. Perhaps even Lenin did not then realize that the new structures being erected were in fact the foundations of a vast totalitarian system."[4]

Problems With the Soviet Government

Government agencies are usually headed by professionals who have experience in the area to be handled by the agency. Someone familiar with finance, for example, would become finance minister; someone who knew about agriculture would become the head of the agriculture department, and so forth. In the new system set up by the Bolsheviks "class considerations took precedence over professionalism"[5]. This created clumsy, inefficient, and often corrupt government. The military, too, became disorganized as a result of many of the same kinds of decisions.

Because the "dictatorship of the proletariat"—which was actually a dictatorship of the Bolshevik party—was more important than day-to-day details, government agencies were not monitored closely to make them more effective. Disorganization in the government led to terrible food shortages and breakdowns of all kinds of essential services throughout Russia. Pressed by liberal and social democratic groups—out of power but still in existence—to hold elections for a Constituent Assembly, Lenin did so. However, when the Bolshevik party did not receive a majority of votes, Lenin simply did away with the Constituent Assembly, just as the tsar had done with the Duma in 1906 and 1907.

The Bolshevik government proceeded to mount a campaign of terror by creating the Extraordinary Commission to Combat Counter-Revolution and Sabotage (Cheka). This new agency was at least as ruthless as the tsar's secret police had been, and it served the same function. It took as prisoners those people who disagreed politically with the Bolsheviks, threatening to execute them if any Bolsheviks came to harm.

To make matters worse, once again, the peasants were starving. By the 1920s, between seven million and nine million children had been orphaned or abandoned because their parents had died or could no longer take care of them.

While trying to figure out how to run Russia, the Bolsheviks still had to deal with the pesky war. World War I was threatening to enter Russia once again. Although Lenin had declared neutrality and an armistice, neither Russia's allies nor its enemies paid much attention. No one but the Germans seemed pleased that the Reds—a name for the Bolsheviks taken from their use of the color red as a symbol—had been unleashed in Russia. While the Allies helped Russian troops against German troops, they also helped counterrevolutionary, or White, troops mobilize to fight against the Bolsheviks. Soon a full-scale civil war was raging in the country. It became apparent to Lenin that World War I, at least for Russia, must be ended.

Peace With Germany

Making peace with Germany proved even more humiliating to the Russians than losing Chinese Manchuria to the Japanese had been. The Treaty of Brest-Litovsk, signed in March 1918 between Russia and Germany, forced Russia to give up a quarter of its territory. This area included the Baltic States, Poland, the Ukraine, part of Byelorussia, and land bordering Turkey. One third of Russia's population, as well as many farms and industries, were located in these areas.

Lenin had no intention of honoring all the treaty's terms. He also hoped, since world revolution was his ultimate aim, that Germany would revolt against its monarchy and join the Bolshevik cause. In the meantime, he was satisfied

Primary Source— From the Peace Treaty of Brest-Litovsk, 1918

Article I. Germany, Austria-Hungary, Bulgaria, and Turkey, for the one part, and Russia, for the other part, declare that the state of war between them has ceased. They are resolved to live henceforth in peace and amity with one another.

Article II. The contracting parties will refrain from any agitation or propaganda against the Government or the public and military institutions of the other party. In so far as this obligation devolves upon Russia, it holds good also for the territories occupied by the Powers of the Quadruple Alliance.

Article III. The territories lying to the west of the line agreed upon by the contracting parties which formerly belonged to Russia, will no longer be subject to Russian sovereignty; the line agreed upon is traced on the map submitted as an essential part of this treaty of peace. The exact fixation of the line will be established by a Russo-German commission.[6]

The areas in black on this map show the territory that Russia gave up as a result of the Treaty of Brest-Litovsk.

to have Russia out of the war. The government moved to Moscow, farther away from possible German attack, taking up headquarters in the walled Kremlin, from which tsars had ruled in the medieval past.

Violence and Disappointment

Violence reigned in the countryside. Bolsheviks were being assassinated by counterrevolutionaries. They, in turn, were killed by Bolsheviks. The new government quickly became as hated and feared as the tsars' had been.

One of the worst tragedies of 1918 was the murder of Tsar Nicholas II and his entire family on July 17. They had been moved to Yekaterinburg, where some former members of the Provisional Government hoped to keep them safe. Fearing the tsar would be a symbol for those who opposed the Bolsheviks to rally around, the party decided it was best to eliminate Nicholas, as well as his wife and children. The entire family was brutally shot and killed in the basement of the house in which they had been staying. Nervous about public reaction, the Bolsheviks leaked the false story that only the tsar had been shot and the rest of the family had been sent away. Perhaps this marked the defining moment at which the Bolshevik Revolution became a force that was willing to ignore human suffering in pursuit of its goals.

Perhaps the revolution can best be summed up in the words of writer Maxim Gorky, once an ardent believer in Lenin and the revolution. In an essay called "Triumph Disappointed," Gorky told of a conversation with an old revolutionary who had told him about a dream he had had:

> Now that I am wide awake I can still see the triumphant people, but I feel that I am a

Tsar Nicholas II and his entire family were executed by the Bolsheviks in 1918.

stranger among them. . . Maybe I, like many others, do not know how to triumph. All my energy went in the struggle; the expectation, the capacity for enjoying possession; is stunted . . .the point is that I see lots of ferocity and revenge about me, but never any joy—the joy that transfigures a man. And I do not see any faith in victory. . . I feel utterly miserable—just as Columbus would have felt if he had reached the coast of America only to find that it was repulsive to him.[7]

CHAPTER 14

Lenin's Legacy

In 1918 Lenin survived two assassination attempts. The first one, on January 14, occurred as Lenin drove through Petrograd following a speech. Protected by a friend in the backseat, Lenin was uninjured by the bullets fired at him. Then a second attempt on his life occurred on August 30. A young revolutionary named Fanny Kaplan shot at him three times while he was giving a speech at a factory. Two bullets hit their target and Lenin dropped to the ground, unconscious.

Rumors flew that he was dead, but he actually recovered faster than was expected. Before she was executed, Fanny Kaplan explained why she had tried to assassinate Lenin. She said she believed he was a traitor to the revolution, and would put the cause of socialism back many years.[1]

After this attempt on his life, Lenin became even more revered by Bolsheviks and their supporters. Terrorist reprisals against "enemies of the state" increased. Full-scale civil war was soon to follow.

Decline in Health and Death

Lenin lived only five more years after this assassination attempt. He suffered a series of strokes that steadily

Although he relied on Joseph Stalin and admired his ruthlessness, Lenin began to distrust his colleague in the years before his death. Stalin would go on to become dictator of the Soviet Union, causing millions of deaths under his regime.

diminished first his physical strength, then his speech. He tried desperately to maintain control over party affairs right up until his third and last stroke. Lenin died on Monday, January 21, 1924.

"The Party leaders saw in the very act of Lenin's burial an enormous opportunity for strengthening the regime," wrote historian Dmitri Volkogonov.[2] At first, Lenin was simply to be buried after a state ceremony. However, a new procedure that mummified bodies (preserved the flesh) had recently been discovered. It was decided to preserve Lenin's body for permanent display to the public. This grisly idea soon took hold, and a huge mausoleum was built in the Kremlin so that Communists could make a pilgrimage to see the legendary leader of the new order.

Stalin's Rise to Power

Before Lenin's death, power had been passing to a handful of top Bolsheviks who were trusted by Lenin: Joseph Stalin was the party administrator; Lev Kamenev managed Moscow; Zinoviev managed Petrograd; and Leon Trotsky dealt with the army, but never having been fully accepted by the Bolsheviks, he fell from power not long after Lenin's death.

Although it took a few years for him to emerge as the party's undisputed leader, by 1927, Joseph Stalin had taken over Lenin's position as the dictator of the Union of Soviet Socialist Republics (USSR), the new name for Communist Russia. Stalin had been very clever at hiding his ruthlessness during his early years as a party leader. Still, before this death, Lenin had begun to distrust him and warned party leaders not to give Stalin great power. Lenin's final stroke so incapacitated him, however, that he was unable to do anything to dilute Stalin's power.

The dream of socialist equality passed, therefore, into the hands of Joseph Stalin. Like Lenin, Stalin believed consistently through his life that the final goal of Marxism— equality for all classes—justified any means to reach that end. This included the mass terror that Lenin had started and that Stalin brought into full being. By the end of Stalin's regime, the USSR would be a nation marked by repression, censorship, and violence against those the government deemed a threat. It was Lenin, with his genuinely admirable

Primary Source—Stalin's Speech on Lenin's Death, 1924

Comrades, we Communists are people of a special mould. We are made of a special stuff. We are those who form the army of the great proletarian strategist, the army of Comrade Lenin. There is nothing higher than the honour of belonging to this army. There is nothing higher than the title of member of the Party whose founder and leader was Comrade Lenin. It is not given to everyone to be a member of such a party. It is the sons of the working class, the sons of want and struggle, the sons of incredible privation and heroic effort who before all should be members of such a party. That is why the Party of the Leninists, the Party of the Communists, is also called the Party of the working class.

DEPARTING FROM US, COMRADE LENIN ENJOINED US TO HOLD HIGH AND GUARD THE PURITY OF THE GREAT TITLE OF MEMBER OF THE PARTY, WE VOW TO YOU, COMRADE LENIN, WE SHALL FULFIL YOUR BEHEST WITH HONOUR![3]

A pro-Communist crowd marches to the mausoleum holding Lenin's body to mark the eighty-fifth anniversary of his death. Today, Lenin remains a significant, if divisive, figure in Russian history.

qualities of courage, determination, intelligence, and single-mindedness, who helped pave the way for Stalin's Terror: "Convinced that their own ideas were the key to the future of the world . . . the Russian intelligentsia divided up the world into the forces of 'progress' and 'reaction,' friends and enemies of the people's cause, leaving no room for doubters in between. Here were the origins of the totalitarian world-view."[4]

Today, the USSR, the world superpower that grew out of the Russian Revolution, has been dissolved. Years of financial troubles and the increasing desire of the people for greater freedom caused the fall of the Soviet system in the late 1980s. Since then, Russia has continued to experience difficulties while reasserting itself as a world power. Vladimir Putin, the President of Russia from 2000 to 2008 and then again from 2012 to today, has received criticism for imprisoning political activists, consolidating his own power, and Russian military intervention in Ukraine (which was part of the USSR, but has been an independent country since its fall). As Lenin learned when he and the Bolsheviks replaced the Provisional Government and the tsarist system, creating meaningful and humane change can be a difficult task.

Fifteen years after the fall of the Soviet Union, the people's wish for a more democratic nation has not yet been completely fulfilled. Much work remains to accomplish what Lenin failed to achieve: "an end to wars, peace among the nations, [and] the cessation of pillaging and violence."[5]

1870—**April 22:** Lenin (Vladimir Ilych Ulyanov) is born in Simbirsk, Russia, on April 22.

1881—**March 13:** Tsar Alexander II is assassinated.

1886—**January 24:** Lenin's father dies.

1887—**May 20:** Lenin's brother, Alexander Ulyanov, is executed.
August 25: Lenin enters Kazan University.
December 17: Lenin is arrested for participation in a student protest demonstration.

1891—Lenin passes law examination at St. Petersburg University.

1892—Lenin works as a lawyer in Samara.

1895—**May–September:** Lenin travels abroad and meets Georgi Plekhanov.
December 21: Lenin is arrested in St. Petersburg.

1897—Lenin starts three-year exile in Siberia.

1898—**March:** Russian Social Democratic Labor party (RSDLP) founded in Minsk, Russia.
July 22: Lenin marries Nadezhda Krupskaya in Shushenskoe, Siberia.

1900—**February 10:** Lenin's exile ends.
March: Lenin arrives in St. Petersburg.
June 3: Lenin is arrested but is released ten days later.
June 29: Lenin leaves Russia to go to Western Europe.

1902—**March:** Lenin's *What Is to Be Done?* is published.

1903—**July–August:** Second congress of RSDLP is held in Brussels, Belgium; the Bolshevik and Menshevik factions split.

1904—**February:** Beginning of Russo-Japanese War.

1905—**January 22:** "Bloody Sunday" takes place in St. Petersburg.
September 5: Peace treaty with Japan signed in Portsmouth, New Hampshire.
October 30: Manifesto signed by Nicholas II, promising civil rights and the Duma.
November 21: Lenin arrives in St. Petersburg.

1906—**May 10:** First Duma opens in St. Petersburg.
July 21: First Duma dissolved; Pëtr Stolypin is appointed prime minister.

1907—**January–April:** Lenin lives in Finland.
December: Lenin moves to Switzerland.
1908—**December:** Lenin moves to Paris, France.
1911—Stolypin is assassinated.
1912—**June:** Lenin moves to Poland.
1914—**July 30:** Russia prepares for war with Germany.
August 1: Germany declares war on Russia.
August 3: World War I begins.
August 8: Lenin is arrested in Austrian Poland.
August 19: Lenin is released.
September: Lenin leaves for Switzerland.
1915—**September:** Tsar Nicholas II takes over as commander of Russian forces.
1916—**December 30:** Rasputin is murdered in Petrograd.
1917—**March 8:** February Revolution begins in Petrograd.
March 12: Formation of Petrograd Soviet.
March 15: Provisional Government is formed; Nicholas II abdicates.
April 16: Lenin arrives in Petrograd.
May: Bolshevik Red Guard is formed.
November 6: Bolshevik Red Guards take over Petrograd.
December 20: Cheka is established.
1918—**January 14:** Assassination attempt on Lenin.
March 3: Treaty of Brest-Litovsk signed between Russia and Germany.
July 17: Tsar Nicholas II and his family are murdered.
1922—**April:** Stalin becomes General Secretary of the Communist party.
1924—**January 21:** Lenin dies. Three days later, St. Petersburg is renamed Leningrad.
1991—Leningrad is restored to its former name, St. Petersburg.

CHAPTER NOTES

CHAPTER 1.   A Revolutionary Beginning

1. Robert Service, *Lenin: A Biography* (Cambridge, MA: Belknapp Press of Harvard University Press, 2000), 254.
2. Richard Pipes, *A Concise History of the Russian Revolution* (New York: Alfred A. Knopf, 1995), 114.
3. V.I. Lenin, "V.I. Lenin to Inessa Armand." *Lenin Collected Works* (Moscow: Progress Publishers, 1976), Marxists Internet Archive, https://www.marxists.org/archive/lenin/works/1917/mar/15ia.htm.
4. Ronald W. Clark, Lenin, *A Biography* (New York: Harper and Row, 1988), 191–207.

CHAPTER 2.   The Ulyanov Family

1. Robert Service, *Lenin: A Biography* (Cambridge, MA1: Belknap Press of Harvard University Press, 2000), 14–16.
2. Dmitri Volkogonov, *Lenin, A New Biography* (New York: The Free Press, 1994), 5.
3. Robert Payne, *The Life and Death of Lenin* (New York: Simon & Schuster, 1964), 46.
4. Ibid., 50.
5. Volkogonov, 11.
6. Payne, 48.
7. Ibid., 49.
8. Ronald W. Clark, *Lenin, A Biography* (New York: Harper and Row, 1988), 11.
9. Ibid.
10. Volkogonov, 12.
11. Payne, 52; Clark, 10.
12. Clark, 14.
13. Alexander Ulyanov quoted in Adam Bruno Ulam, *The Bolsheviks: The Intellectual and Political History of the Triumph of Communism in Russia* (Boston: Harvard University Press, 2009), 11.

CHAPTER 3.   The Seeds of Revolution

1. Bertram D. Wolfe, *Three Who Made A Revolution* (Boston: Beacon Press, 1948), 18.

2. Richard Pipes, *A Concise History of the Russian Revolution* (New York: Alfred A. Knopf, 1995), 14.
3. Ibid., 4.
4. W. Bruce Lincoln, *In War's Dark Shadow* (New York, Cambridge, MA: The Dial Press, 1983), 50.
5. *Polnoe sobranie zakonov Russkoi Imperii (Complete Collection of the Laws of the Russian Empire)*, 2nd series, no. 36490, vol. 36, 130–134.
6. Wolfe, 64.

CHAPTER 4. A Revolutionary Is Born

1. Dmitri Volkogonov, *Lenin, A New Biography* (New York: The Free Press, 1994), 18.
2. Ibid., 19.
3. Karl Marx, "Capital, Volume One," in *The Marx-Engels Reader*, 2nd ed., ed. Robert C. Tucker (New York: W.W. Norton & Company, 1978), 326.
4. Karl Marx and Friedrich Engels, "Manifesto of the Communist Party," *The Marx-Engels Reader*, 2nd ed., ed. Robert C. Tucker (New York: W.W. Norton & Company, 1978), 500.
5. Harold Shukman, *Lenin and the Russian Revolution* (New York: Capricorn Books, 1968), 25–26.
6. Elyse Topalian, *V.I. Lenin* (New York: Franklin Watts, 1983), 28.
7. Bertram D. Wolfe, *Three Who Made A Revolution* (Boston: Beacon Press, 1948) 85.
8. W. Bruce Lincoln, *In War's Dark Shadow* (New York: The Dial Press, 1983), 18–19.
9. Volkogonov, 27.
10. Ibid., 26, 27.

CHAPTER 5. Lenin in Exile

1. Esther Kingston-Mann, *Lenin and the Problem of Marxist Peasant Revolution* (Oxford: Oxford University Press, 1983), 45.
2. Dmitri Volkogonov, *Lenin, A New Biography* (New York: The Free Press, 1994), 24.
3. Richard Pipes, *A Concise History of the Russian Revolution* (New York: Alfred A. Knopf, 1995), 31.

4. Volkogonov, 31–32.
5. V.I. Lenin, "Letter from V.I. Lenin to his mother," *Lenin Collected Works* (Moscow: Progress Publishers, 1977), 174–175.
6. Ronald W. Clark, *Lenin, A Biography* (New York: Harper and Row, 1988), 32.
7. Ibid., 34.
8. Henry M. Christman, ed., *Essential Works of Lenin: "What Is to Be Done?" and Other Writings* (New York: Dover Publications, Inc., 1987), 148.
9. Pipes, 106.

CHAPTER 6.   Growing Pains in the Party

1. "The Life and Work of V.I. Lenin (1900)," Marxists Internet Archives, https://www.marxists.org/archive/lenin/works/lifework/worklife/1900.htm.
2. Robert Service, *Lenin: A Biography* (Cambridge, MA: The Belknap Press of Harvard University Press, 2000), 135.
3. Bertram D. Wolfe, *Three Who Made A Revolution* (Boston: Beacon Press, 1948), 145.
4. Ibid., 146.
5. Ibid., 145.
6. Service, 132–133.
7. Dmitri Volkogonov, *Lenin, A New Biography* (New York: The Free Press, 1994), 1.
8. Ibid., 50.
9. V.I. Lenin, "Declaration of the Editorial Board of Iskra." *Lenin Collected Works: Volume 4* (Moscow: Progress Publishers, 1964), Marxists Internet Archive, https://www.marxists.org/archive/lenin/works/1900/sep/iskra.htm.
10. Ibid., 55.

CHAPTER 7.   The Road to Revolution

1. Richard Pipes, *A Concise History of the Russian Revolution* (New York: Alfred A. Knopf, 1995), 35.
2. Robert Service, *Lenin: A Biography* (Cambridge, MA: The Belknap Press of Harvard University Press, 2000), 167.
3. Pipes, 39.

4. Ronald W. Clark, *Lenin, A Biography* (New York: Harper and Row, 1988), 101–102.
5. Pipes, 40.
6. Ibid., 41.
7. Ibid., 42.
8. *Polnoe sobranie zakonov Rossiiskoi Imperii (Complete Collection of the Laws of the Russian Empire)*, 3rd series, no. 26803, vol. XXVI.

CHAPTER 8.   Stunted Reforms

1. Harold Shukman, *Lenin and the Russian Revolution* (New York: Capricorn Books, 1968), 79.
2. Ibid., 81.
3. Ibid.
4. Bertram D. Wolfe, *Three Who Made A Revolution* (Boston: Beacon Press, 1948), 335.
5. Shukman, 81.
6. Robert Service, *Lenin: A Biography* (Cambridge, MA: The Belknap Press of Harvard University Press, 2000), 169–170.
7. V.I. Lenin, *Selected Works* (Moscow: Progress Publishers, 1975), vol. 1, 529–534.
8. Service, 178–179.
9. Ukaz of 9 November 1906, "On Peasants Leaving the Land Commune," from *The Stolypin Agrarian Reform*, http://cla.calpoly.edu/~mriedlsp/history315/Documents/stolypin.html.

CHAPTER 9.   The Great War

1. Elise Topalian, *V.I. Lenin* (New York: Franklin Watts, 1983), 78.
2. Dmitri Volkogonov, *Lenin, A New Biography* (New York: The Free Press, 1994), 105.
3. Bertram D. Wolfe, *Three Who Made A Revolution* (Boston: Beacon Press, 1948), 53.
4. V.I. Lenin, "Lecture on the 1905 Revolution," Lenin's Collected Works: Volume 23 (Moscow: Progress Publishers, 1964) Marxists Internet Archive, https://www.marxists.org/archive/lenin/works/1917/jan/09.htm.

Chapter Notes

CHAPTER 10. The February Revolution

1. Richard Pipes, *A Concise History of the Russian Revolution* (New York: Alfred A. Knopf, 1995), 77.
2. Elise Topalian, *V.I. Lenin* (New York: Franklin Watts, 1983), 82.
3. Richard Pipes, *A Concise History of the Russian Revolution* (New York: Alfred A. Knopf, 1995), 80.
4. Ibid., 81.
5. Ibid., 82–83.
6. Ibid., 84.
7. "Abdication of Nikolai II, March 15, 1917," *The Times*, March 19, 1917, https://community.dur.ac.uk/a.k.harrington/abdicatn.html.
8. Pipes, 80.
9. V.I. Lenin, "Speech Delivered at a Meeting of Soldiers of the Izmailovsky Regiment," *Lenin's Collected Works: Volume 24* (Moscow: Progress Publishers, 1964), Marxists Internet Archive, https://www.marxists.org/archive/lenin/works/1917/apr/10.htm.

CHAPTER 11. Lenin's Rise to Power

1. Dmitri Volkogonov, *Lenin, A New Biography* (New York: The Free Press, 1994), 121.
2. Ronald W. Clark, *Lenin, A Biography* (New York: Harper and Row, 1988), 210; Volkogonov, 140.
3. Richard Pipes, *A Concise History of the Russian Revolution* (New York: Alfred A. Knopf, 1995), 117.
4. Harold Shukman, *Lenin and the Russian Revolution* (New York: Capricorn Books, 1968), 178.
5. Pipes, 115.
6. Sheila Fitzpatrick, *The Russian Revolution* (Oxford: Oxford University Press, 2008), 51.
7. V.I. Lenin, "The Tasks of the Proletariat in the Present Revolution," *Lenin's Collected Works: Volume 24* (Moscow: Progress Publishers, 1964), Marxists Internet Archive, https://www.marxists.org/archive/lenin/works/1917/apr/04.htm.
8. Pipes., 120.
9. Fitzpatrick, 84.
10. Volkogonov, 139.
11. Pipes, 127.

12. Volkogonov, 140.

CHAPTER 12. The October Revolution

1. Richard Pipes, *A Concise History of the Russian Revolution* (New York: Alfred A. Knopf, 1995), 136.
2. Ibid.
3. Ibid., 137.
4. Harold Shukman, *Lenin and the Russian Revolution* (New York: Capricorn Books, 1968), 192.
5. Ibid., 183.
6. Pipes, 139.
7. Paul Halsall, "Lenin: Call to Power, Oct 24, 1917," *Modern History Sourcebook*, August 1997, http://www.fordham.edu/halsall/mod/modsbook39.html.
8. Pipes, 139–140.
9. Ibid., 145.
10. Ibid.
11. Ronald W. Clark, *Lenin, A Biography* (New York: Harper and Row, 1988), 272–273.
12. Ibid., 274–275.
13. Orlando Figes, *Revolutionary Russia: 1891–1991* (New York: Metropolitan Books, 2014), 91.
14. V.I. Lenin, "To the Citizens of Russia!" *Lenin's Collected Works: Volume 26* (Moscow: Progress Publishers, 1972), Marxists Internet Archive, https://www.marxists.org/archive/lenin/works/1917/oct/25.htm.

CHAPTER 13. The Bolsheviks Take Over

1. Harold Shukman, *Lenin and the Russian Revolution* (New York: Capricorn Books, 1968), 8.
2. Dmitri Volkogonov, *Lenin, A New Biography* (New York: The Free Press, 1994), 162.
3. Ibid., 163.
4. Ibid., 167.
5. Ibid., 166.

6. "The Peace Treaty of Brest-Litovsk," *The WWI Internet Archive*, accessed June 29, 2015, http://wwi.lib.byu.edu/index.php/The_Peace_Treaty_of_Brest-Litovsk.
7. Maxim Gorky, "Triumph Disappointed," *Fragments from My Diary* (Middlesex, England: Penguin Books, 1972), 199.

CHAPTER 14.   Lenin's Legacy

1. Dmitri Volkogonov, *Lenin, A New Biography* (New York: The Free Press, 1994), 224.
2. Ibid., 436.
3. J.V. Stalin, "On the Death of Lenin." *Selected Works*, (Albania: The "8 Nëntori" Publishing House, 1979), *Marxists Internet Archive*, https://www.marxists.org/reference/archive/stalin/works/1924/01/30.htm.
4. Orlando Figes, *A People's Tragedy: The Russian Revolution: 1891–1924* (New York: Penguin Books, 1998), 127.
5. V.I. Lenin, "The Question of Peace." *Lenin's Collected Works: Volume 21* (Moscow: Progress Publishers, 1974), Marxists Internet Archive, https://www.marxists.org/archive/lenin/works/1915/jul/x02.htm.

GLOSSARY

autocracy—A government that is ruled by one person with total power.

Bolsheviks—Led by Lenin, this radical faction of the RSDLP fought for revolution in Russia.

bourgeoisie—Middle-class business owners.

capitalism—The economic system in which businesses are owned and run by private individuals, leading to competition in a free market.

communism—A social and economic system in which property is shared between all members of a community or state.

constitutional monarchy—A form of government in which a king or queen governs with a parliament and his or her powers are restricted by the constitution.

coup—The overthrow of an established government.

Duma—An elected legislature, created by Tsar Nicholas II in 1905.

feudalism—A social system in which the nobility was given land from the monarchy and peasants were forced to live on and work their lord's land in exchange for protection.

Ispolkom—The executive committee formed in 1917 to unify and organize soviet groups and run the government.

Mensheviks—The more moderate faction of the RSDLP that believed that violence could be avoided through democratic means.

proletariat—The working class.

Russian Social Democratic Labor Party (RSDLP)—The communist party that fought for revolution in Russia and split into two separate parties: the Bolsheviks and the Mensheviks.

serf—A peasant who, under feudalism, was bound to live and work on his lord's estate.

Soviets—Representative governmental bodies, meaning "council" in Russian, that were set up during the Russian Revolution.

tsar—The emperor of Russia.

Zemstva—Local government institutions set up by Tsar Alexander II to end feudalism.

FURTHER READING

Books

Allen, John. *The Russian Federation: Then and Now.* San Diego: Referencepoint Press, 2014.

Fleming, Candace. *The Family Romanov: Murder, Rebellion, and the Fall of Imperial Russia.* New York: Schwartz & Wade, 2014.

Lih, Lars T. *Lenin.* London: Reaktion Books, 2011.

Maier, Corinne. *Marx.* London: Nobrow Press, 2014.

Murphy, John. *Socialism and Communism.* New York: Rosen, 2014.

Websites

Russian Revolution
www.history.com/topics/russian-revolution
The History Channel presents an overview of the Russian Revolution along with several short educational videos.

Lenin Internet Archive
www.marxists.org/archive/lenin/index.htm
Website includes Lenin's works, biography, images, and audio.

Vladimir Lenin
www.biography.com/people/vladimir-lenin-9379007
Provides an account of Lenin's life as well as several videos.

INDEX